ℳORE THAN PETTICOATS

———⟫●◦⟪———

REMARKABLE OHIO WOMEN

Greta Anderson

TWODOT®

GUILFORD, CONNECTICUT
HELENA, MONTANA
AN IMPRINT OF THE GLOBE PEQUOT PRESS

Dedicated to my teachers at CSG:
Dorothy Sehring, Eleanor Wagner,
Flora Sedgwick, Jack Guy, Daniel Hall,
and in memory of Charles Wong.

A · TWODOT ® · BOOK

Copyright © 2005 by The Globe Pequot Press

All rights reserved. No part of this book may be reproduced or transmitted in any form by any means, electronic or mechanical, including photocopying and recording, or by any information storage and retrieval system, except as may be expressly permitted by the 1976 Copyright Act or by the publisher. Requests for permission should be made in writing to The Globe Pequot Press, P.O. Box 480, Guilford, Connecticut 06437.

TwoDot is a registered trademark of The Globe Pequot Press.

Library of Congress Cataloging-in-Publication Data
Anderson, Greta.
  More than petticoats. Remarkable Ohio women/Greta Anderson.—1st ed.
    p.cm.—(More than petticoats)
  Includes bibliographical references and index.
  ISBN 0-7627-3625-9
  I. Women—Ohio—Biography. 2. Women—Ohio—History. 3. Ohio—
  Biography. I. Title: Remarkable Ohio women. II. Title. III. Series: More than
  petticoats series.
  CT3262.O3A53 2005
  920.72'09771—dc22

                                                                      2005046068

Manufactured in the United States of America
First Edition/First Printing

Contents

ꙆNTRODUCTION

I have many memories of my years at the Columbus School for Girls, a private K–12 institution that, with its perpetual re-enactment of time-honored "school traditions," seems—at least it did in my years there—almost designed to create memories in its student body. Of course what I remember has little to do with those traditions, as I played and felt the rebel as much as I dared and never saw "tradition" as a thing to be revered. Perhaps the role of women was changing so fast that I felt I had no ties to women of the past. If so, I was wrong. In any event, as I wrote this book, two otherwise inconsequential C.S.G. memories pushed themselves into my consciousness and were so persistent that I finally prom-ised myself to give them room in this introduction.

In Ohio, regrettably, as in many other states, the subject of the state's history is relegated to fourth-grade social studies—a good indicator of how little our educational system fosters regional awareness, despite its prime importance to our economic and cultural lives. It was the same when I was growing up in Ohio. "Memorize the state motto, and move on" was the message.

Fourth grade was my first year at C.S.G., and I had the best of all teachers, Mrs. Sehring. She was a large woman with power-ful ideas and a firm but gentle voice. She taught us chess. She allowed us to raise mice in the classroom. She directed our class in a version of *Hamlet*. When she read to us, we were spellbound. Mrs. Sehring smiled and saw possibilities and made school entertaining. When it came to Ohio History, however, she just showed us the book. I realized this as I was writing these biographies; then I remembered the book itself. It was workbook-like, of cheap, pulpy paper. It was dense, and it was dull. I distinctly remember sitting before it at my desk, plowing through the endless paragraphs, getting nowhere, then returning to reread the same impenetrable text, about fossils or Iroquois or the seven so-so presidents. I yearned for the period to end, yet I knew I had learned nothing. The whole thing made me feel profoundly deficient.

The fact is that, unless history is story, it becomes mere duty, a state-ordered task. I suppose Mrs. Sehring considered teaching Ohio History a "duty" and dispensed with it accordingly. Soon enough the half-hour was over, and we were back to charting the lineage of our mice, drawing posters of some famous artwork, or practicing our lines from *Hamlet* ("Something is rotten in the state of Denmark"). My desire in this book was to make stories and drama of the distaff side of Ohio history (and if it's drama you seek, start with Victoria Woodhull). It was to write a book that a teacher like Mrs. Sehring might want to read aloud, or retell in bits and pieces (and if you are reading aloud to children, you might want to skip Victoria!). It was to entertain and instruct, with the emphasis on "entertain" (and you are encouraged to skip any biographies here that don't meet that standard!).

The second C.S.G. memory dates to my junior year, when I took a class called Women and Literature from Mrs. Sedgwick. She warned us at the outset that our readings would comprise more books *about* women than *by* women, possibly because her favorite nineteenth-century author was neither Austen nor the Brontës nor Eliot, but Thomas Hardy. I do not regret my time spent with *Tess of the D'Urberville's:* The tale of that long-haired country lass quite carried me away. Mrs. Sedgwick loved drama, too; so we read *The Taming of the Shrew* and Ibsen's *A Doll's House* and *Hedda Gabler*. By

Introduction

women authors, we read Sylvia Plath's *A Bell Jar* and Virginia Woolf's *A Room of One's Own.*

Clearly I must have loved this course, or I could not list the readings now, almost twenty-five years later. And indeed, they are a fine set of readings—unless you happen to notice that more than half of them are by or about suicides. I did notice, partly because of my history—my grandmother was a suicide, and I was said to possess her smile and her love of writing—and partly because I connected deeply with the stories of "self-immolation," a word I am sure I learned from Sedgwick.

My memory involves writing the final exam. I even know where in the auditorium I sat. Sedgwick's tests were always easy to prepare for; you simply constructed an outline of the points she had emphasized, memorized the outline, then wrote out paragraphs when the time came. This exam was different. It asked us to write an essay on the question, "What did you learn?" I turned my answer into a diatribe against the course content. Women and Literature should not be Women's Suicide and Literature. It should not be Literature by Men about Women. Surely there were some female authors who did not commit suicide. Surely a woman could be something other than a victim, a sexual manipulator (Hedda), or the butt of a good joke ("the Shrew"). Even Nora of *A Doll's House* was no kind of role model!

I felt satisfied when I turned in that blue book, and for the first time in my C.S.G. career, I did not care what grade I received. I had struck upon something important to me. I was looking for role models, for some sense of path or purpose. We girls heard encouragement all around: "You can be anything you want: doctors, lawyers, engineers." The truth was, I needed to know more. Those were just professions. What could women *do* with their lives? What was—and is—*important* for women to achieve? And how do they go about achieving it?

Introduction

Writing this book of biographies and the previous two books I have written in this series has helped me find answers to those questions. The women in these biographies found ways to live out larger visions. Through their thoughtful and committed action, they helped point the way to the promise of a richer, more meaningful humanity. I hope you, my readers, find their signposts as useful as I have.

HARRIET BEECHER STOWE
1811–1896

"The Little Lady Who Made a Big War"

*T*he Beechers' wagon jostled over Ohio's "corduroy roads"—logs laid side by side to make the mud passable. So this was "the West"! Harriet's father, the Reverend Lyman Beecher, and her older sister, Catharine, were a bit dreamy-eyed about their mission in this land, but the twenty-one-year-old Harriet was wide awake and curious, albeit sad to be leaving childhood friends behind. She noted the fine soil, the gentle contours of the land, and the easy simplicity of the dwellings, and compared them to the rocky landscape and upright, buttoned-down abodes of her native New England. Everything was new to her, and she liked its newness.

The year was 1832, and Cincinnati was the family's destination. Reverend Beecher, a prominent clergyman—one of the biggest names in the religious revival known as the Great Awakening—had been appointed to head the Lane Theological Seminary and had been self-appointed to "cure" the West of Catholicism and unbelief. Like a biblical patriarch commanded to enter a foreign land, he led into this wilderness his second wife, his sister,

Harriet Beecher Stowe

and his children, who ranged in age from Catharine, thirty-two, to Isabella, ten, and James, four. In between were Harriet, twenty-one, and her favorite brother, Henry Ward, nineteen. It has been said that these two—the most famous of this famous brood—learned the most from their time in the Queen City.

In that era, Cincinnati was a study in contrasts. Nestled among the hills surrounding the junction of the Ohio River and several smaller rivers, it had a grace and nobility that earned it the nickname. In 1832 it was beginning to boom, with a population of 25,000 up from 10,000 in 1820—a figure that would reach 114,000 in 1851. Cincinnati prospered during the era of steamboat travel and became Ohio's first big city. As a convenient distribution point, it had become the hog-processing capital of the world, turning Ohio's agricultural riches into ready cash. The "smell of money" pervaded the city's unpaved streets, as free-roving pigs rambled, gobbling up the garbage that people left out in piles for them. Hence, the Queen City was also Porkopolis. It smelled, it sweltered, and it bred disease.

What shocked Harriet far more than the sights and smells of hogs was her sudden proximity to the realities of America's "peculiar institution." Across the river from Cincinnati was the slave state of Kentucky, and its slaves were in high demand. The mechanization of cotton processing in the early 1800s had spurred demand for raw cotton, picked by slaves in the hot sun of the Deep South. Because the importation of slaves from Africa had been outlawed since the turn of the century, slaveholders' estates in more northern states like Kentucky had become the main source for this precious commodity. Never before had more human flesh changed hands in the region.

Until now for Harriet slavery had been a philosophical and political issue. The abolition movement to free the slaves, though by no means yet a popular cause even in New England, was nonetheless a frequent topic of discussion in the educated class to which her family belonged. While her older brothers favored it, her father and Catharine opposed the abolitionists for seeming too ready to accept a violent solution. Although Harriet could see both sides, she tended to favor her brothers' views.

But slavery could not be kept at arm's length in Cincinnati. It was a horrible and obtrusive fact. Harriet was aghast to pick up the newspaper and read advertisements in which "Negroes" were listed together with mules, carts, bedsteads, and saddles. Or, likewise, to read offers by traders to pay cash for "likely young Negroes." What, wondered Harriet, would become of the children or parents of these "likely" laborers as their dear ones were sold downriver? As she settled into Cincinnati, she began unconsciously collecting stories—from domestic servants, friends, acquaintances, newspapers, even from strangers overheard in public places—all bearing upon this subject that simultaneously repulsed and riveted her. She watched as the controversy increasingly stirred the community around her. Then, in 1851–52, just one year after Harriet returned to the East, these stories and observations would flow forth onto the manuscript pages of what became the most widely read and most influential novel in American history, *Uncle Tom's Cabin.*

Harriet Beecher was born in Litchfield, Connecticut, in 1811, the seventh child of the Reverend Lyman Beecher and his capable, intelligent first wife, Roxana Foote Beecher. Roxana bore two more children, Henry and Charles, before dying of consumption in 1816 at the age of forty-one. Fortunately for young Harriet, her namesake and spinster aunt, Harriet Foote, a vigorous woman, embraced the task of raising her. Thus, Harriet was brought up in two households: one, the simple, pious, and often tumultuous household of her siblings and her Congregational father; the other, the more worldly, upper-middle-class household of her mother's family.

One can imagine it would be hard for a "middle child" to stand out in a family of nine siblings—and more, counting the children from the reverend's second marriage. But Harriet made it her business to stand out. In fact her very nature was exceptional: She was labeled odd by some; genius by others. She enjoyed chopping wood with her brothers; best of all was the moment when, having wheeled the load of wood back with them, she would hear her father exclaim that she should have been a boy. While her sister Mary received straight A's at the Litchfield Female Academy, Harriet's performance was far more uneven: She would rather listen to what the older children were learning from Mr. Brace—the dynamic schoolteacher who boarded at her house—than attend to her own lessons. To join this group, she volunteered to do the advanced writing assignments. After two years an essay by Harriet on the difficulty of proving the soul's immortality was featured at the school's annual students' exhibition. As the essay was read aloud, eleven-year-old Harriet studied her father's face, detected sure signs of kindled interest, and thrilled when he turned to Mr. Brace to ask whose work it was.

"Your daughter's, sir," was the answer to the proud patriarch.

Harriet was not the only talented Beecher daughter. In 1823 Catharine Beecher opened the Hartford Female Seminary, essentially a college for high school–aged girls. The seed for this grand scheme was Catharine's disappointment with how little she had gained academically from her Litchfield education, which predated Mr. Brace's arrival at the school. She worried that, even with Mr. Brace's influence, Harriet's intellectual progress would end with graduation. Hence, she recruited Harriet, thirteen, to be "assistant pupil" in a system in which the advanced girls taught the younger ones. Harriet's first assignment was to master Latin so that she could teach it to others. This subject was particularly symbolic: Though common in boys' schools, Latin was a subject considered too rigorous for female minds.

Harriet had another interesting assignment at the school, shared by many of her schoolmates—in fact, by all who had experienced religious conversion: It was to introduce her un-churched peers to the articles of the Christian faith and to convert them if at all possible. Though startling today, such a mandate was common in the days of the Great Awakening. To this end the Christian students received special instruction on how to influence others. Harriet carried out her ministry primarily through letters to friends. Rather than preach to them from on high, as her father was wont to do, Harriet conducted her correspondence as a conversation between equals, eliciting and shaping her friends' views in a tone of hushed confidence.

After graduation in 1827 Harriet returned to her father's household, now in Boston. Without the company of friends and with few opportunities to employ her mind, Harriet despaired, writing to Catharine: "I don't know as I am fit for anything, and I have thought that I could wish to die young, and let the remembrance of me and my faults perish in the grave, rather than live, as I fear I do, a trouble to everyone." The obvious remedy to Harriet's melancholy was for her to rejoin Catharine at Hartford, where she was greatly needed as a teacher. This was her role from 1827 to 1832, when the family headed west. Harriet enjoyed teaching those students who wanted to learn, but did not feel the call as strongly as her sister. If anything, teaching wore her out. When Catharine proposed they open a female seminary in Cincinnati, Harriet responded with tepid agreement, hoping that something more interesting might come her way.

Once in the Queen City, Harriet gravitated to her uncle Samuel Foote as the likeliest source of that something interesting. Foote had moved to Cincinnati several years earlier, started the local water concern, and, having profited handsomely, built a mansion on a bluff overlooking the city. In his previous life as a ship's captain, Foote traveled the world, bringing back trinkets and tales to his adoring young nieces and nephews in Connecticut. Now, gatherings at the Foote mansion provided the overworked schoolteacher an agreeable respite from the serious sense of purpose that seemed to pervade all things Beecher. It was there that Harriet first encountered the Semi-Colon Club, a literary club comprised mostly of transplanted New Englanders. When a geography textbook Harriet had written for her students was published in both her and Catharine's names, they were invited to join.

Such clubs were common in cities of the antebellum era; their purpose was to provide their members an evening's entertainment and the satisfaction of creating a written work. The Semi-Colon Club gathered weekly in the parlor of a member's home to hear each other's latest essays and poems, to debate current issues, to dance, and occasionally to drink. This friendly forum provided ample encouragement for Harriet's first literary forays, many of them satirical. One club member encouraged her to submit her writing to his literary journal, the *Western Monthly* magazine. She agreed, on the condition that her name be withheld from print. One of these early contributions won a literary prize.

It was at these weekly gatherings that Harriet became acquainted with her future husband, Calvin Stowe, through a close friendship with his attractive wife, Eliza. The Stowes were fellow New Englanders, and the Reverend Stowe was a colleague of her father's at the Lane Theological Seminary. In the summer of 1834, while Harriet was back East visiting her grandmother, a deadly wave of cholera claimed Eliza's life. When Harriet returned, her response to Calvin's grief was less pious than that of the others; she alone seemed to accept his emotional upheaval as natural and not to be repressed. His dependence on her grew into love, and a marriage proposal came several months later.

Harriet, born and bred to be an independent-minded woman, was never less sure of her future than on her wedding day early in 1836. She wrote to her cousin Georgiana May, "Well, my dear G., about half an hour more and your old friend, companion, schoolmate, sister, etc., will cease to be Hatty Beecher and change to nobody knows who." Her life did change, drastically. She had to give up teaching, which she had not thoroughly relished, but which at least had provided a sense of professional achievement. In addition she was soon expecting a child. Her first pregnancy resulted in twin girls, later named Eliza and Harriet. All of these changes she experienced alone, as Calvin took care of professional duties on an extended trip to London.

Calvin was a brilliant academic who was often overwhelmed by the practical world. He needed a capable woman to look after everything from his mental health to his finances. Harriet proved to be such a woman, as well as being his intellectual peer. As the marriage continued to produce offspring—after the twins, a son Henry, another son Frederick, and a daughter Georgiana, all within the space of seven years—Harriet began to supplement his salary with her own earnings. In the late 1830s and early 1840s, she wrote dozens of stories for such widely circulated publications as *Godey's Lady's Book* and the *New York Evangelist.* No longer the literary ingénue, Harriet signed her own name to these pieces, which focused on life in New England. The stream of paychecks steadily increased, and it became a point of pride for Harriet that she could, with her own earnings, hire a housekeeper to free her from three hours of household duties each day. She wrote a friend, "I have determined not to be a mere domestic slave"—an interesting choice of words, to be sure.

The demand for supplementary income stemmed from a crisis at Lane dating back to 1834, when Lyman Beecher came out on the wrong side of a racial controversy. While Beecher and Stowe were back East raising funds, Theodore Weld, the publisher of an abolitionist newspaper whose presses were destroyed several times in riots that rocked the city, organized the theology students to hold a public debate on the topic of slavery. Abolition carried the day, and the impassioned students subsequently pledged to serve Cincinnati's black community in what amounted to an inner-city reading program. The rest of the city abhorred this notion, causing Lane's trustees to outlaw public meetings and discussions of abolition altogether. Rev. Beecher enforced this ruling, clearly in violation of the students' rights. In protest, forty Lane students left for Oberlin College, where Beecher's rival—the greatest name of the Great Awakening, Charles G. Finney—taught. Lane Seminary only limped along thereafter, barely able to pay its renowned scholars their much-reduced salaries.

The "peculiar institution" touched Harriet's life in other ways. The servant who freed her from her own domestic slavery came to her by way of a Kentucky plantation. Harriet was shocked to learn that Matilda, raised as a slave, had never heard of Jesus Christ. Another shock came when Matilda informed Harriet that her former master was in Cincinnati, looking for her: Though she was legally free, no legal body could or would defend her against his claim. Action was required immediately. Calvin volunteered to drive Matilda ten miles down a winding dirt road and across a creek into the woods where a known abolitionist, John Van Zandt, resided. This incident, typical of the Underground Railroad in Ohio, would reappear as part of the character Eliza's story in *Uncle Tom's Cabin.*

Harriet had, with a friend, visited a Kentucky plantation in 1834. She had silently noted the contrast between the rough-hewn slave cabins and the mansion where she was received. She marveled at the sumptuous feast served to her and at the graces of a light-skinned house servant. She watched as the slave-owner commanded his slaves to perform some evening's entertainment for them. All of these scenes and details became part of her book.

But that would not be for another decade. The 1840s were a tumultuous time for Harriet. She was nearing the age her mother had been when she died and seems to have believed her own death was near. In 1843 her brother George committed suicide; her daughter Georgiana, born several weeks later, was a weak and colicky child. In 1844 the struggling family was forced to take in boarders to help make ends meet, disrupting whatever domestic harmony Harriet could hope to achieve; the next year Harriet was laid low by cholera. She recovered and, after a miscarriage, bore a healthy son, Samuel Charles, her hope and joy. Little Charley's death of cholera the following year came as the last and worst blow in this time of trials.

Only Harriet's renewed faith saw her through these calamities. In 1843 she underwent a more emotional conversion than the one she had professed as a teen. Following the pattern established for such events in that era, Harriet's spiritual rebirth was preceded by a sense of utter helplessness, questioning, and fatigue from the exertion of her own will. When "self-despair was final, then came the long-expected and wished-for help." Harriet wrote, "My *all* changed."

It was a critical moment for Harriet. Today, someone reading *Uncle Tom's Cabin* would feel it to be as much a call to Christian faith as an indictment of slavery. Uncle Tom, the book's central character, is himself clearly a Christ figure, whipped to death in the end, but not before his example frees the slaves of his former Kentucky plantation. The book is riddled with heart-rending religious speeches by him and by the white child, Eva, a character whose sweetness and suffering and death also enable those around her to experience the truth of Christ's universal love. Stowe's dual purpose—the passion of her dual commitments to social change and spiritual renewal—brought her book into the hearts of the American public. The pain she felt at the loss of her own innocent one was the fire that tempered her imagination.

The resolve to write the book came two years after Samuel Charles's death, after Harriet had left Cincinnati—its muddy streets and dirty water, its high society and hidden poverty and its explosive racial tension—all the much wiser for her experience. When Calvin received an offer from Bowdoin College in 1849, Harriet, pregnant again, returned east with three of her children to set up house in Maine. On the way she visited siblings in Brooklyn, Hartford, and Boston. Everyone wanted to talk politics, mostly to decry the proposed Fugitive Slave Act, which would make it illegal to feed, clothe, or shelter a runaway slave—which would in fact *require* Northerners to assist in their capture.

Harriet's spirit was braced by this debate and the righteousness of her brothers' positions. Soon thereafter the birth of her child, whom she named Charles, ended her period of mourning for the first Charley. When the Fugitive Slave Act was passed as part of the Compromise of 1850, Harriet fired off letters to all of her siblings, inciting them to protest: "Must we forever keep calm and smile and smile when every sentiment of . . . humanity is kicked and rolled in the dust and lies trampled and bleeding. . . ?" She followed the stories in the newspaper of alleged runaways being hauled off to the South, despite all evidence that these Northern black men were legally free. Finally, a sister-in-law wrote her from

Boston, "Hattie, if I could use a pen as you can, I would write something that would make this whole nation feel what an accursed thing slavery is."

Legend has it that Harriet read this letter to her children, then, rising from her chair, pronounced: "I will write something. I will if I live." Five months later, in June 1851, she submitted the first of what would be forty installments to the *National Era,* an abolitionist weekly.

Harriet accomplished exactly what she had set out to do. *Uncle Tom's Cabin: or, Life among the Lowly* popularized the abolition cause worldwide by its insistence on the humanity of African Americans. The reader is led to identify with the slave characters and to celebrate their courage, whether it is Eliza with her infant daughter crossing the Ohio River by leaping from ice floe to ice floe, her proud husband, George, deceiving the slave catchers with his refined speech and manners, or the ill-used Cassy conceiving a perfect plot to escape her tormenter, Simon Legree. Even Uncle Tom, whose deep humility became distorted by caricature in later years, exemplifies this trait when he refuses to abandon his values to appease Legree's vicious will. While the heroes of the book are slaves, most of the slaveholders are portrayed sympathetically. The primary evil of slavery shown in the book is not the cruelty of masters, but the systematic separation of families—husband from wife, infant from mother. Harriet attempted to place the blame on slavery itself and not on those who benefited from it. The exception is Legree, introduced late in the book's pages, whose heinous character reflects unmitigated evil.

How popular was Harriet Beecher Stowe's novel? Within the first year, the book had sold 300,000 copies—at a time when the nation's total population, including children, was fewer than twenty-five million. Though the book was banned in the South, virtually every literate household in the North owned the two-volume set, and each set was shared by numerous readers. Harriet's royalty check after three months was $10,000, then the largest amount ever received by an author in the English-speaking world. Soon stage versions of the book were conceived, bringing the story to even more people. *Uncle Tom's Cabin* sold very well in Britain and was translated into thirty-seven languages. Harriet Beecher Stowe was an overwhelming success, the name on everybody's tongue.

Southerners protested the work vigorously, denying its veracity, but the tide of public opinion had turned against the institution they sought to defend. Harriet merely sharpened her quills and published *A Key to Uncle Tom's Cabin*, which catalogues the sources of her fiction in published slave narratives, newspaper clippings, and personal experiences. This book, too, was a bestseller. When President Lincoln met her several years later, he greeted her with the famous lines, "So you're the little lady who made this big war." One might quibble with respect to Lincoln's tone, as others have taken umbrage with Stowe's depiction of blacks. But his message was no exaggeration. *Uncle Tom's Cabin* changed—or at least hastened—the course of history.

Catapulted into wealth, Harriet could now travel the world and enjoy life in the style of her Uncle Samuel, and she built a mansion in a fashionable neighborhood of Hartford. Her troubles were not over, though. The mansion proved impractical to maintain and the Stowes were forced to call it a loss. Her alcoholic son Frederick coaxed his parents into another bad investment, an orange grove in Florida, then vanished on a trip out west. In fact none of Harriet's children, whom she had labored so hard to raise, lived full, happy lives—with the sole exception of the youngest, Charles. Meanwhile, Harriet's career was beset with bad publicity. Taking the side of Lady Byron against her husband, the notorious poet Lord Byron, she wrote a book that exposed Byron's incestuous relations with his half-sister. The book received public scorn.

Then, scandal rocked her own family, when Henry Ward Beecher crossed swords with another Ohio heroine, the journalist Victoria Woodhull, who exposed his adultery with a parishioner. Regardless of her reputation, Harriet continued to turn out best-selling and influential works; her nonfiction book on Florida, *Palmetto Leaves* (1873), literally created a land boom in that state.

Melodrama and tragedy did not tarnish Harriet's dignity—or dampen her sense of humor. At age seventy-five she was described by a Scottish clergyman as "a wonderfully agile old lady, as fresh as a squirrel still but with the air of a lion." She enjoyed the friendship of her Hartford neighbors, the poet Oliver Wendell Holmes and especially Mark Twain, who amused her with his mordant wit. And Calvin Stowe had remained a true friend and faithful companion all their married years. When he died, her health began to suffer. Ten years later, in 1896, she passed away and was buried beside him in the Andover Chapel Cemetery in Massachusetts.

Eliza Jane Trimble Thompson

1816–1905

Mother of a Crusade

*E*liza Trimble Thompson could not decide whether or not to attend the temperance lecture of Dr. Diocletian Lewis. As a member of the Methodist Episcopal Church, Eliza deplored liquor and its effects. But Lewis was promoting a particular course of action about which Eliza, as a prominent citizen of Hillsboro, had great reservations. At any rate, she and her husband, Judge Thompson, had gotten the gist of the talk at last night's dinner table, as Lewis was staying as a guest in their home.

After Dr. Lewis left for the Hillsboro Music Hall (the "doctor" was an unofficial epithet from the Homeopathic Hospital College of Cleveland), husband and wife began talking. The judge was of the opinion that "the whole business [was] tomfoolery." Eliza was partially inclined to agree and finally remained at home, while her twenty-four-year-old daughter, Mary, and nineteen-year-old son, Henry, both satisfied their curiosity and went to the lecture. Over 150 people attended the assembly on December 23, 1873.

Lewis began his talk by pointing out what seemed obvious to many in the audience. They had seen for themselves that, without strong measures, intoxicating liquor would become the ruin of society. Alcohol made working men idle and good women slatternly; it corrupted marriages and cursed families with legacies of sorrow. Then, Lewis launched into the original part of his talk. He retold the dramatic story of his mother and her friends in Clarksville, New York—how in 1853 they had descended *en masse* upon pharmacies, hotels, and saloons; how they had begged the owners to cease their sales of alcohol; how they had prayed aloud to

Eliza Jane Trimble Thompson

God for the power to turn these men's hearts to His service; and finally, how they had succeeded in their mission.

Lewis looked out at his audience and suggested that such a ministry might work there in Hillsboro, if only the women had the proper crusading spirit. He addressed them. "How many of you will go forth to the places where liquor is sold?" Seventy women bravely stood.

Then he addressed the men. "How many of you will stand behind them and support them in what they do?" About the same number of men rose.

It was decided that the group would meet the following morning at the First Presbyterian Church to choose a leader and begin its campaign.

In the Thompson household, not much was said until the following morning, after Dr. Lewis left for Washington Court House, where he would deliver his next address. The children reported the remarkable developments to their mother and told her that she herself had been mentioned as one of the prominent women in town who could lend credibility to the women's efforts.

Mary asked her mother tentatively, "Mother, will you go to the meeting this morning?"

Eliza replied that she did not yet know.

Sensing the gravity of the decision she must make and not wishing to impose his will, her husband said, "Children, let us leave your mother alone, for you know where she goes for all vexed questions."

Alone, Eliza kneeled and had just begun to turn her thoughts to prayer when she heard a tap on the door. It was Mary, holding the family Bible. "Mother, I opened to the 146th Psalm, and I believe it is for you."

As Eliza read, the significance of the psalm washed over her. It opens with a call to put matters into God's hands as "there is no help" in men. True enough: Men's laws had done nothing to change evil ways. "The Lord looseth the prisoners." *The prisoners of drink,* thought Eliza. "The Lord openeth the eyes of the blind: the Lord raiseth them that are bowed down" *The very same.* Then, building to its climax: "The Lord loveth the righteous; The Lord preserveth the strangers; he relieveth the fatherless and widow—but the way of the wicked he turneth upside down."

With new resolve, Eliza donned her winter cloak and went out into the chilly December air. "This is the way; walk ye in it," she declared to herself, and her footsteps took her directly to the church door.

Eliza Trimble was born in 1816 in Hillsboro, Ohio. Little is known of her mother, Rachel Trimble, except that she assumed her husband's role as the clerk of Highland County's court of common pleas during the War of 1812. The year Eliza was born, Allen

Trimble was elected to the Ohio House of Representatives. He then served two terms as an Ohio senator. In these roles, he was instrumental in the building of the state's canal system, which became the key means of transporting Ohio's agricultural goods to market. In 1822 he served one year as acting governor of the state; then, in 1826 he was elected Ohio's tenth governor and served two terms.

Of Allen Trimble's seven children, Eliza was the only girl, and he doted on her, perhaps to a degree that it became public knowledge. A story illustrates this. The day he took office as acting governor, a prisoner's wife appeared with a request for her husband's pardon, which, after reviewing the case, Trimble denied. Shortly thereafter, the prison warden visited Trimble and inquired whether he had a six- or seven-year-old girl. The governor replied that he had, Eliza Jane. The warden then reported the prisoner's boast that his wife's sister aimed to get employment as a hired girl at Thompson's home in order to kidnap Eliza in revenge for Trimble's decision. The governor sent an urgent message home, and Eliza was closely protected thereafter.

Trimble also wrote frequent letters to Eliza when, at age twelve, she left home to study at Pickets Academy in Cincinnati. He expressed worry that Eliza would study so hard as to injure her health. He also pressed upon her the duty she owed her Creator. A new convert to the Methodist Episcopal Church, which preached among other things abstinence from alcoholic beverages, he became the first president of the Ohio State Temperance Society in 1829, while he was still governor. In 1836 when Eliza was twenty, they attended an American Temperance Society Convention together in Saratoga.

The next year, Eliza married James Henry Thompson, a lawyer from Kentucky whose brother was a United States senator. They moved into a large, graceful Hillsboro house built by Trimble—no doubt to keep his sole daughter nearby. It is easy to see why Eliza was considered a woman of high standing in the town. Still, most of Eliza's adult life was given over to bearing and raising children. Between the years of 1838 and 1854, she gave birth to eight children and raised the seven who survived. She was a petite, almost frail, woman who seemed destined to fade into obscurity—until circumstances thrust her into history's limelight.

When Eliza entered the Presbyterian Church on the morning of Christmas Eve 1873, the meeting was already under way. She quietly took a seat at the back of the church, but was immediately noticed by the others and was asked to be their leader. She was willing. Shortly thereafter a man rose and spoke to the other men present: "Brethren, let us adjourn and leave this work to God and the women."

The departure of the men had a stimulating effect upon the women. Psalm 146 was read. One woman, the wife of General Irvin McDowell (of Civil War fame), led a prayer, and according to Eliza, "the 'tongue of fire' sat upon her, and all were deeply affected"; another woman said it was as if an angel had brought down a live coal from heaven. The wife of Eliza's Methodist minister began the hymn "Give to the Winds Thy Fears," and the women spontaneously processed out of the church, two by two, with Eliza at the head. Among all, wrote one participant, was an eerie calm of purpose: "No crowd of shouting boys followed, or cliques of consulting men on the street corners were gathered, every countryman halted his team in awe. No vociferous or angry words were heard, and no officer commanded the peace—for it was a death-like peace."

They stopped at the first of the three drugstores they would visit that day. Eliza addressed the druggist: "I suppose you understand the reason of our visit." She then continued:

"As you look upon some of the faces before you and observe the marks of sorrow caused by the unholy business that you ply, you will find that it is no wonder why we are here. We have come however, not to threaten, not even to upbraid but in the name of our Divine Father and Savior, and in his spirit to forgive and to commend you to his pardon, if you will but agree to abandon a business that is so damaging to our hearts and to the peace of our homes. Let us pray."

The women kneeled, and Eliza led them in a fervent prayer for the soul of the man standing before them.

The druggist readily signed the pledge that had been composed the night before, and the women continued on to the next drugstore, where they met with the same success. It was at the last drugstore, owned by a Mr. Dunn, where they encountered their first opposition. Dunn refused to be "prayed at," and he refused to sign their pledge. His trade in liquor, he felt, was perfectly legal; as the existing law stipulated, he never sold to minors, habitual drunks, or those who were intoxicated. The women retired for the day, but did not give up on Mr. Dunn.

On December 27 the Hillsboro women took on their most challenging opponent—the saloons. This action took more than ordinary courage. It defied the ordinary behavior expected of women, and this is why Eliza's respectability was so important. According to a Cincinnati *Gazette* reporter (who was probably not present):

> They went with trembling limbs and anxious hearts. It was to them a strange experience, a new idea. It seemed subversive of all recognized rules of womanly conduct. The thought of going into the low part of the town and entering one of those vile dens which respectable people abhorred at a distance; of kneeling in sawdust and filth, and pleading with bloated and beery saloon-keepers,

was overwhelming to their finer sensibilities and shocking to their modesty. They shrank from the task half in doubt and half in fear.

Then, according to the newspapermen, they turned their minds to the effects of drunkenness upon homes, families, and children, and "their misgivings left them, and personal considerations no longer had any weight."

The Hillsboro women had only moderate success. One saloonkeeper responded by pouring all of his liquor onto the street, but not all were so moved. Another saloonkeeper, Mr. Beck, agreed to sign the pledge, but only if it were presented to him by men. In Washington Court House it was a different story. Led by Matilda Gilruth Carpenter, the women who had heard Dr. Dio Lewis on December 24 took action Christmas Day. By January 2, 1874, every business in town that had previously sold alcohol had pledged to cease doing so. In early 1874 the Woman's Temperance Crusade, as it became known, spread from Hillsboro and Washington Court House to the Ohio towns of Wilmington, Greenfield, Xenia, Mt. Vernon, New Vienna, and South Charleston.

One of the tactics of the Washington Court House women was to erect a "tabernacle" outside the doors of a recalcitrant liquor dealer and hold an ongoing vigil to shame him into compliance. It was a case of "love the sinner, hate the sin"; or, in the words of one journalist, "It was whiskey selling they were fighting against, not the whiskey seller." And so the Hillsboro women attempted the same with their recalcitrant druggist, Mr. Dunn, though probably without Eliza, whose scruples would not likely condone such theatrics and whose name is not associated with the action. At any rate, Dunn was not converted. He responded to his plummeting sales by gaining a temporary injunction against the tabernacle and filing a $10,000 damage suit against the women. The court eventually ruled in his favor, though it decreased his reward to $5 plus his lawyer's fees.

Nonetheless, it was the inspired action of the women of Hillsboro—not the achievements of women elsewhere in the state—that Dr. Dio Lewis extolled on his winter lecture tour. Within fifty days the liquor traffic was driven from 250 Ohio towns. By April 1874 the time had come to organize on a larger scale. Women from the various local chapters met in Cincinnati and formed the Ohio Woman's Christian Temperance Union. In November of the same year, temperance women from eighteen states gathered in Cleveland to form the national WCTU, the organization that finally achieved its prime objective in 1920 with the enactment of the Eighteenth Amendment prohibiting the sale and production of alcohol—an amendment that was revoked in 1933.

At the first meeting of the WCTU, the claims of both Hillsboro and Washington Court House as the birthplace of the movement were debated. Other women had organized on December 22 in Fredonia, New York, where Dr. Lewis had spoken the week before he came to Ohio. Eliza addressed this issue directly: "God chose Hillsboro as the birthplace of the Crusade." Her proclamation—her conviction, rather, of a Pentecostal occurrence—seemed to decide the matter. Eliza Thompson, then fifty-eight, won the appellation Mother Thompson and was thereafter considered the founder of the crusade, and thus, a key founder of the WCTU.

In fact organized opposition to alcohol had taken shape much earlier in the century. The American Temperance Society was formed in 1826, giving rise to more than 2,000 local temperance societies, most of them in New England. The fervor migrated west to Ohio with the avatars of the Great Awakening, Charles G.

Finney and Lyman Beecher. In Ohio temperance fever manifested itself in destructive episodes: In 1856 some ladies in Albany forcibly poured out the stock of a local liquor dealer; and in 1865 women residents wrecked the local whiskey shops in Greenfield. Later, after the formation of the WCTU, the Ohioan Lucy Hayes, or "Lemonade Lucy," became one of the nation's most famous temperance advocates by banning liquor from the White House during her husband's presidency.

Mother Thompson had no official position in the WCTU, although she attended several conferences and spoke at some of them. While younger women ran the organization, Eliza played a symbolic role to its membership. In her daughter Mary's words, "the tender word 'Mother' was wrenched from her home and given to the world." Eliza received countless letters from women "confiding Joys and Sorrows to a mother's heart," and presumably she responded with due care and attention. In 1903 the annual WCTU conference was held in Cincinnati and included a pilgrimage to Hillsboro to visit Eliza's home and the church "where it had all begun." With her snowy white hair under a cap, and a white shawl wrapped around her frail shoulders, Mother received the stream of guests graciously.

Part of Eliza's grace lay in her modesty and in her knowing when modesty was due. Approaching her death, this woman who had risked her good reputation one December day and became the icon of a movement ultimately preferred a gentler, truer tune: "My dear children and friends, when the chariot swings low enough for me to step in, let all things be done quietly, modestly and humbly; no display. Saved by grace must be my theme on earth and my theme in heaven." Eliza Jane Trimble Thompson died in 1905 at the age of eighty-nine, preceded in death by her husband and six of her children and survived only by her two youngest sons.

MARY ANN BALL BICKERDYKE

1817–1901

The Nurse Who Outranked General Sherman

$\mathcal{F}$ollowing the July 1863 victory at Vicksburg, the Union soldiers under the command of Ohio-born generals Ulysses S. Grant and William T. Sherman were given a brief reprieve. Most of the men traveled home; some invited their families to come see them. One colonel's wife brought their nine-year-old son, who promptly caught the measles. Seeking the best possible care, she came to hear of one Mother Bickerdyke, a nurse who practically ran the field hospital and who was known for a quality of medical care that far exceeded the military's low standards on that score, and so she sought her out at the hospital.

Having heard the woman's request and sized up the situation, Mrs. Bickerdyke made no secret of her conclusions. Could this lady not see that she was busy—dressing wounds, changing linens, overseeing the preparation of palatable food for the wounded and dying? This child had nothing but ordinary measles, which any mother should know how to treat; the hospital patients had bullet wounds and amputated limbs. What was she thinking,

Mary Ann Ball Bickerdyke

anyhow, bringing a nine-year-old to a war zone? War was no Sunday excursion. Now, if only this lady would kindly get out of the way, she could get back to work.

The colonel's wife was shocked into tears and ran to the arms of her husband. The colonel proceeded immediately to General Sherman's tent to report the behavior of the "nasty old woman" at the hospital. When the "nasty old woman" was identified, Sherman's response was a hearty guffaw. "Mother Bickerdyke?" he said. "I'm afraid I can't help you there. Unfortunately, you've found the one person around here who outranks me. If you want to lodge a complaint against her, you'll have to take it to President Lincoln."

This story became one of the many legends surrounding the famous Civil War nurse of the western campaign, Mary Ann Ball Bickerdyke. She was beloved by common soldiers and generals alike and disliked only by those mid-level officers and surgeons who resented her utter disregard of protocol and her refusal to be impressed by their authority. They were cowed by her unfailing common sense, which—to the credit of the Union Army—invariably won out over their bureaucratic conceits. Mary Ann Bickerdyke served much of her time in the army as an unpaid volunteer. When she was asked "on whose authority" she was acting—whether ordering privates about or requisitioning goods from the Army supply warehouse—her standard answer was: "The Lord God Almighty."

So, Mother Bickerdyke did outrank Billy Sherman. But she gave credit where it was due: "It takes a big man like him to say so."

Mary Ann Ball, the first child of Hiram and Annie Rodgers Ball, was born in Knox County on a farm along the Kokosing River, then known as Owl Creek. Annie died a year later. Though Hiram remarried, most of the rest of Mary's childhood was spent on a Richland County farm her Grandpa Rodgers had claimed after serving in the Revolutionary War. John Chapman—the legendary Johnny Appleseed—had planted the Rodgerses' apple orchard. Mary loved the outdoors and came to know much of the common herbal lore through her Grandma Rodgers. Somehow—probably in a one-room schoolhouse—Mary learned to read and write. What Mary did not learn was the polished language and feminine restraint cultivated in upper-class urban women. Her female colleagues in the war took note of her rough manners and made them part of the Mother Bickerdyke legend.

After the death of her maternal grandparents, Mary stayed on with a Rodgers uncle, who eventually moved to Cincinnati. Cincinnati would also become Mary's destination. But at age sixteen she sought a different kind of adventure, arriving in Oberlin, Ohio, in 1833, the year that John Shipherd founded the institution that became the nation's first coeducational college. Oberlin College records show no sign of her matriculation, and it is hard to imagine where she would have found money for tuition. Yet it is possible that she was employed in the household of a faculty member or audited classes for free. She spent four years in Oberlin, and it is certain that she broadened her horizons while living there.

Mary moved to Cincinnati in 1837 at the age of twenty. There, in the same chaotic, cholera-plagued city where Harriet Beecher bore six of her seven children, Mary is believed to have studied homeopathic medicine at a small "physio-botanic" institution. In contrast to the male-dominated conventional medicine of the time, which favored invasive measures such as bloodletting, blistering, surgery, amputation, and calomel treatments, homeopathic medicine welcomed women practitioners and taught the skillful use of native herbs, fresh air, and hot water, as well as diets abundant in fruits and vegetables. Several years later, after Mary left Ohio, she hung out a shingle as a "botanic physician" and became known by her community as a skilled practitioner.

In 1847 Mary married Robert Bickerdyke, an immigrant from Yorkshire, England, and a widower with two boys and a girl. The family, soon augmented by the birth of two more boys, scraped by on Robert's earnings as a self-employed sign painter. Robert's real passion was music. In 1851 he had the opportunity to tour the country as a musician for Jenny Lind, the sensational Swedish Nightingale, but turned it down for the family's sake. Mary, who had little interest in music, operated a section of the Underground Railroad, transporting runaway slaves to a Quaker home in Hamilton in her husband's paint-spattered wagon, which came to be used less and less as either his work or his will to work dried up. In 1856 the struggling family moved to Galesburg, Illinois, to join Robert's brother. There, Robert enjoyed a brief local prominence as a musician, then died in 1859, leaving Mary to support herself and her two boys on her earnings as a botanic healer.

The real turning point in Widow Bickerdyke's life came during one Sunday morning worship service at Galesburg's First Congregational Church. The church's pastor was Harriet Beecher's older brother, Edward, who lacked none of the famous Beecher flair. For this particular Sunday in the spring of 1861, he used as the "text" of his sermon a letter from Dr. Benjamin Woodward, a Galesburg physician who had answered the first call for volunteers and was stationed at Cairo, Illinois, where the Ohio and Mississippi Rivers meet and where units of the Union Army were encamped. Woodward's letter described how dozens of soldiers were dying of dysentery, pneumonia, and typhoid—without even having encountered hostile fire. The hospital tents were filthy, the army surgeons considered the soldiers' complaints trifling, and the only "nurses" were convalescents who spared themselves every effort on others' behalf in the hope of getting well themselves. The Reverend Beecher read the entire letter, with its urgent request for supplies and its list of Galesburg boys among the afflicted. He then asked his congregation, would they care to proceed with the regular Sabbath worship or suspend worship to address the situation at Cairo?

The sentiment was unanimous: "When your ox falls into the pit, you dig him out first and pray afterward." One woman offered, "What them boys need is their mammies." She had a point. "Women's work"—cooking, cleaning, doing laundry—did much to keep families healthy. The army, being strictly male, lacked these skills and inclinations. The female nursing profession had yet to be invented, largely because most medical care was still delivered at home, by mothers and wives. Indeed, hospitals at the time were more like asylums, warehouses for people whose illness made them inconvenient to others.

Reverend Beecher suggested instead that the community send another physician with the needed supplies. The man they chose should have good medical judgment, moral character, and the determination needed to stand up to military authorities. The "man" who was nominated, and then unanimously selected, was Mary Ann Bickerdyke, a mother and a physician with an uncompromising attitude. She agreed, if they'd promise to look after her boys. "I'll clean things up down there, don't you worry. . . . This is the Lord's work you're calling me to do. And when I'm doing the Lord's work, they ain't nobody big enough to stop me," she said.

Mary Ann Bickerdyke arrived in Cairo wearing her plain gray calico dress. It had rained heavily the night before, and the air was humid and hot. Dr. Woodward greeted her with the news that he had secured a "day's pass"; she would need to leave by sunset. "We'll see about that" was her answer. In the first hospital tent, she saw ten men lying side by side on straw pallets. Their clothes were soaked with perspiration and encrusted with vomit; the mud floor was befouled with human excrement. There was no water in the drinking pail. The men moaned and shivered, and the air stank. A few men sat listlessly by. Mary inspected every hospital tent, but they were all like this.

Mary needed some manpower, so she marched over to the campfire where some privates were roasting salt pork and eating hardtack. "Not very good eating, I'd say. A piece of fried chicken would go better. And some lightbread with blackberry jam." She could fix that kind of grub, if they would go help the captain with a few jobs, like getting some water boiling. Then she entered the first tent and ordered everybody out for a bath. Afterwards they could dress themselves in the fresh shirts and drawers she'd brought. Finding a couple of shovels and a helper, she mucked out the tent, scraping it down to a clean, dry base. Clean straw was found to make fresh pallets. This process was repeated with the other tents as she prepared the food she'd brought from Galesburg. By sunset, everyone was washed and fed and tucked into clean beds. She gave each tent of men its own pep talk about taking care of themselves and each other.

Dr. Woodward thanked her for her trip, assuming that she was to take the evening train back to Galesburg. But Mary Ann Bickerdyke had no such intention. She'd be back tomorrow, you could be sure of that! As she left camp to find a suitable place in town to stay, one of her helpers said, "Goodnight, Mother." Soon the entire western army would know her by that name.

Mary returned the next day and the next. She immediately made up a wish list for the folks in Galesburg: soap, underwear, chamber pots, blankets, quilts, kettles, skillets, and a washboard. In a short time the Sanitary Commission would be established for such provisions, but for now these arrangements were in her hands alone. Five other regiments were stationed in Cairo, each with its own filthy hospital camp. Mother Bickerdyke charged into each situation and got the same response: heartfelt gratitude from the men and dismay, if not disgruntlement, from the doctors.

After the Battle of Belmont, Cairo had its first real wounded, and a local hotel was converted into a hospital. The chief surgeon quickly commandeered the building and kicked Mary out. She could help with the laundry, if she liked. But Mary knew that there are many ways of doing battle. She agreed to relinquish the cooking duties—as long as they were done right. They weren't, of course. The specialty goods sent for the sick men—preserves, whiskey, clean clothes—were soon being filched by the hospital cook and his cronies. So Mary set a trap. One afternoon, she stewed some dried peaches for the sick men, adding sugar, cinnamon, and a secret ingredient. "Never mind me," she indicated to the cook. "This is just for my boys." She set platters of the peaches on the windowsill to cool, their heavenly fragrance wafting in the summer breeze. Then she left the room. Within just minutes, a chorus of retching sounds was heard from behind the kitchen doors. Triumphant, Mother confronted the filchers, assuring them that the tartar emetic they had ingested was harmless, but that their thievery was not. Eventually, the chief surgeon was transferred, and with the blessings of General Grant, Mary took unofficial charge of hospital personnel.

In January 1862 Grant easily captured Fort Henry on the Tennessee River and planned his move downriver to Fort Donelson, where a grueling three-day battle took place in February, producing the largest number of casualties so far in the western campaign. Mother Bickerdyke hitched a ride to the site on the Sanitary Commission's "floating hospital," the *City of Memphis*. Men who had been frozen to the ground in pools of their own blood were carried to the barge, half-dead. Mother sponged them off, got them into clean, dry clothes, warmed them up, fed them, and nursed them back to life. She was told that all the living had been brought in from the battlefield, but even after a full day's nursing, she could not rest. At midnight she went out with a lantern to see for herself. The story of Mother Bickerdyke's midnight search was told by newspapers and made her a public figure. But this battle and its gruesome aftermath decided her fate in other, more important ways. Rather than return to Cairo, which had straightened out considerably since she first arrived, she would continue to serve where she was needed. As her biographer puts it, "Without consulting anyone, she calmly attached herself to Grant's army. When it moved south, she moved with it."

This "not consulting anyone" became a pattern for Mary. When she needed a kettle for boiling hospital laundry, she swapped Sanitary Commission tea with local women. When she needed meat for a tasty stew to revive her boys, she told a local "secesh" dealer to bill it to the Sanitary Commission. When she needed firewood to keep her boys warm, she persuaded some privates to dismantle an old fortification. When her boys needed a rest along one of the long, hard marches, she bellowed out, "Halt!" in her best "general's voice," and the company halted. Her boys were the sick and wounded, and what they needed, they would get.

Mary's freedom came in part from her willingness to do the dirtiest jobs. The medical director at Memphis disliked sick people and disliked meddling women. He assigned Mary to the army pest house at Fort Pickering, a "hospital" for smallpox patients. In addition to the sick, attended only by one another, nine dead men lay rotting there for want of burial. Mary calmly accepted the post. The dead were buried, the floors were scrubbed, the walls whitewashed, and a new latrine dug. Without interference from medical personnel, she quietly instituted botanic remedies, treating her patients with black root, goldenseal, sassafras tea, and beet juice. Given this kind of care, many men survived; at the very least, they died a less gruesome death.

In the end, the Sanitary Commission had little recourse but to hire her. It certainly could not get rid of her. But Mother Bickerdyke was not for sale and initially resisted their offer of employment. She relented only when she considered what kinds of extras the salary could buy for her boys. Her resourcefulness and popularity served the commission well. For instance, rather than depend on low-quality "secesh" milk, she solicited Northern farmers for donations of dairy cattle, which traveled with the troops. At one point during the war, the Northern women decided to send all their pickles and sauerkraut south with the commission, convinced that vinegar, being sour like limes, could prevent springtime scurvy. Mother, however, was not convinced, and neither was General Sherman—in Ohio, one simply ate spring greens—and she intervened to make sure the pickles remained in Chicago and that the precious cargo space be filled with bandages instead.

On one trip to Chicago to meet Mary Livermore, the head of the Northwest Sanitary Commission, Mary Ann Bickerdyke was invited to join her hostess at a fashionable wedding party—the kind of function old women in calico usually do not attend. The groom recognized her instantly and introduced her to his guests as the woman who had saved his leg. Indeed, Mother often hid men with treatable leg and arm wounds from the surgeons, who seemed to prefer amputation to all other treatments. Mother Bickerdyke entertained the wedding guests for hours with her stories, a performance that—at the behest of Mrs. Livermore—she repeated throughout the region, raising funds and supplies for the cause so dear to her: her boys. As for her own biological sons, James and Hiram, she managed on this trip to place them in a Chicago boarding school run by a Presbyterian minister and his wife.

Mother Bickerdyke's most captivating fund-raising performance came late in the war, in Brooklyn. Having made her scheduled appeals in the New York area, Mother decided in her free time she would like to attend a sermon by the great Congregational minister, Henry Ward Beecher. One can imagine her in her calico, seated among Brooklyn's most fashionable ladies, themselves clothed in yards and yards of the finest silk and muslin. When she was recognized and asked to speak after church, a curious idea struck her. Nothing was needed at the front more than bandages; there were never enough. She agreed to speak—but to the women only. She described the needs of the field hospitals, then abruptly changed the subject to the current fashion of wearing layered petticoats rather than hoops. "How many of you is wearing two petticoats, raise your hands." Every hand in the audience went up. "Keep 'em up if you're wearing three." Most of the women, it turned out, were wearing five petticoats. Mother Bickerdyke then asked them to imagine her bandaging a soldier's bloody stump with a gunnysack. She reminded them that she herself was a mother, and a good

Congregational woman like them. "Now stand up, all of you. Lift your dresses," she commanded. The women stood with skirts lifted, laughing nervously. "Ladies of Brooklyn, in the name of my boys, drop that fifth petticoat!" she ordered. And thus, Mother Bick-erdyke departed Brooklyn with a sizable bundle of fine white muslin.

Mother was a woman who got things done, and the Union generals knew and appreciated this. If food was needed some-where, they could count on her to make arrangements. When the war was over, the Union troops gathered in Washington for a vic-tory celebration. Mary put in a parade appearance, riding along-side General Logan on her horse, Old Whitey; then she was asked to join General and Mrs. Sherman in the V.I.P. section to view the parade. Mother demurred. She didn't care much for parades; she had work to do. No one else had thought to feed her boys! She had a tent ready with sandwiches and lemonade, and that's where she would be.

For several years after the war, Mary ran a home in Salina, Kansas, that fed and housed war veterans as they sought to get started farming land claims. With her friend Billy Sherman's assis-tance, she won financial backing from the Kansas Pacific Railroad. The Ohio farm girl gave crack advice on raising crops. However, she could not quite orient herself to the pursuit of profits, and the railroad foreclosed on her otherwise thriving venture. Eventually, her reputation for results led to other employment. In 1870 she was called to New York to serve on the Protestant Board of City Missions. Her assignment was to hand out tracts and "bring peo-ple to Jesus." What she actually did was to scrub and launder and groom and boss the slums' immigrant population into decent liv-ing. She did this with all the vigor and good judgment she had applied to hospital sanitation: threatening abusive parents with the workhouse, hounding jail inmates to improve their ways, and herding children to Sunday school. There was little room to dispute her methods; still less, her motives.

Mary was due for a rest. After four years in New York, she quit her job to join her sons, who were establishing a farm in Kansas. That was 1874, the year of the great locust plague that denuded the land. This crisis spurred Mary into action again, petitioning friends and acquaintances across the country to help her with "grasshopper relief." As a result of her efforts, 200 railroad carloads of food and clothing were shipped and distributed in Kansas. Finally, she collapsed from exhaustion and was sent to California for a rest cure. Up and down the coast she encountered countless old friends, including many disabled war veterans who had been denied their pensions. Assuming power of attorney for at least a dozen, she boarded the new transcontinental railroad in San Francisco and headed to the nation's capital to resume her heroic battle with bureaucratic red tape. She asked nothing in return for her trouble.

When Mary Ann Ball Bickerdyke finally recognized that her life and work could not go on forever, she turned to girlhood memories of Ohio. Letters to her cousin Nellie Ball of Fredericktown reminisced about the sugar camp and the creek where she used to wade. When Nellie visited her in Kansas late in 1897, she brought a barrel of maple sugar and some buckeyes, as if to lure Mary back. It worked. Word spread that Mother was coming home, and every Ball and Rodgers family across Ohio invited her to stay. She visited cousins in Cleveland, Mt. Vernon, Fredericktown, and Mansfield and on many farms in between. A large Ball family reunion was held on Thanksgiving, and the December arrival of her son Jimmy, by then a high school principal in Kansas, occasioned another round of visits throughout Knox and Richland Counties. Then

Jimmy took her home to his cottage in Kansas, where she remained until her death in 1901.

A statue in Galesburg, still standing, and a World War II freighter were the only public memorials to Mary Ann Bickerdyke. Few have heard of this woman who "outranked Sherman," while most know of Clara Barton, the pioneering Civil War nurse of the eastern campaign who founded the American Red Cross. None of that would have mattered to Mary. The memorials that mattered to her lived in the memories of her Civil War boys and were put to rest with them.

VICTORIA C. WOODHULL

1838–1927

Avatar of Free Love and the Vote

$\mathcal{S}$an Francisco in the 1850s had been a land of opportunity for Victoria C. Woodhull—if you count upscale prostitution an opportunity. There were few other opportunities available to lower-class women in the pre-Civil War era. As a seamstress earning a mere $3 a week, Victoria had met an actress who offered to introduce her to the stage. Victoria was beautiful, with a dramatic flair and a knack for memorizing texts. She instantly became a regular in the shows—and at the parties that followed the shows. That was where the men in the audience went when they found one of the girls onstage to their liking. Victoria's increased wages—fifty-two dollars a week—sufficed to support her morphine-addicted husband and her toothless, imbecile six-year-old son.

Victoria knew she was "meant for some other fate."

By her account, Victoria was onstage when her younger sister, Tennessee, appeared before her in a vision, saying: "Victoria, come home!" And again: "Come home!"

In 1860 "home" was Ohio.

Victoria slipped offstage and, in full costume, ran to her lodgings and began packing. The next day, she, her husband, and

Victoria C. Woodhull

their son, Byron, boarded a steamer for the East Coast. When they arrived, by train, in Ohio, sister Tennie was wearing the same dress she had been wearing in the vision, so the story goes.

It had been years since Victoria had lived with her family, but they had not changed. Tennessee, age fourteen, the youngest child of Buck and Roxana Claflin's large brood, was now the family's main breadwinner. Her powers of clairvoyance made her a road-show attraction at a time when Spiritualism—communicating with the dead—and Magnetism—using the body's electrical fields for healing purposes—were fast-growing sensations throughout the country. Buck played the huckster, marketing an alcohol-and-morphine concoction as Miss Tennessee's Magnetic Life Elixir, and collected information from cemetery headstones to assist in Tennie's supposed contacts with the dead. The rest of the family spent their energies squabbling over the proceeds.

Victoria had married precisely to escape this kind of exploitation. In her youth, she too had been a clairvoyant bread-winner for the Claflin family—often deprived of food to make her more susceptible to visions. Back among them at age twenty-two, she now had an ally in Tennie. She also felt allied with the women who came for her Magnetic cures: women who had been sexually abused by their fathers, as had Victoria; women who wished to escape their marriages, but could not; women who felt sexual desires, then considered a disease in women. Victoria began to connect her story to theirs, to see a pattern in the economic relations between men and women and a double standard in the sexuality deemed proper for the two genders. Ten years later, these realizations would make Victoria Woodhull the most scandalous name in the country.

Victoria was the seventh of Roxana Claflin's children—a fact that the unschooled, superstitious mother, prone to speak in tongues at Methodist revival meetings, believed to be lucky. Roxana even claimed that Victoria had been conceived at a revival: While all around her fell to the ground in swoons and she herself proclaimed having been "born again in the Lamb's blood," Buck allegedly dragged her to the back of the tent and performed the fateful act.

The year of Victoria's birth was 1838, a time of national economic crisis, also the year Buck's luck as a wheeling and dealing real estate man began to run dry. Growing up in Homer, Ohio, Victoria would know the disappointment of poverty and the social ostracism born of her family's oddities. When she was five, the family was run out of town when Buck's unprofitable gristmill—his only remaining business property—burned to the ground in a suspicious fire.

Mt. Gilead, Ohio, was the family's next home. It was there that Dr. Canning Woodhull was summoned when Victoria "fell ill" at the age of fourteen. The "ailment" from which she suffered was pregnancy, compounded by the despair of knowing that Buck was the child's father. In Victoria's words, her "sorrow was ripening her into a woman." No wonder that, when Dr. Woodhull declared, "My little puss, tell your father and mother that I want you for a wife," the young teenager readily agreed. Buck refused to relinquish her, so she and the doctor eloped to Chicago.

The doctor was only a marginally better husband than Buck was a father. Nightly he would leave the young bride for the tavern and brothel. Some nights he returned; some, not. He was drunk when Victoria gave birth to Byron, and absent three days later when she nearly succumbed to childbed fever—at which point Roxana mysteriously appeared in person, "sent by the spirits" to care for her. Hoping that California would cure Woodhull of his drunkenness, Victoria took the family to San Francisco. Between them she was the only one who would find opportunity there.

Dr. Woodhull proved to be the same besotted father when the child was his own. Victoria's second childbirth, in 1861, took place in a rented room in New York City. In one short year after returning from San Francisco, they had left Ohio for Indianapolis, been evicted by their landlady, and traveled to New York seeking to sponge off Woodhull's father. During the birth, the inebriated doctor/husband botched the cutting of the umbilical cord; when Victoria awoke, the bed was a pool of blood. Miraculously, the baby, whom she named Zula Maud, survived. Three days later, she saw Dr. Woodhull through her window, staggering up the stairs to a house across the street he obviously thought was theirs. At that point Victoria finally asked, "Why should I any longer live with this man?" She moved back to Ohio—this time, alone.

How did Victoria manage to survive the nightmare of her youth? Around age seven, she received a special vision. Her best friend in Mt. Gilead, Rachel Scribner, had just passed away. Victoria stood in the Scribners' apple grove, unable to cry, when Rachel's spirit descended, took her by the hand, and rose with her on a spiral path through intense white light into the spirit world. Victoria met spirits whom she would later know by name. They told her that she had special work to do on earth and that they would guide her to it. They showed her a panoramic vision of the future, of mountains and valleys changing places, chaos and panic giving way to beauty and calm. In the end, earth became a paradise, indistinguishable from heaven. Both as an escape from this world's pain and as her hope for a grander fate, this vision stayed with Victoria throughout her life.

In 1865, now in St. Louis, Victoria took the first step on her journey and found herself a decent husband. A handsome hometown hero, Colonel James Harvey Blood of the Union Army was also an ardent follower of Spiritualism. When he consulted the new medium in town, the "entranced" Victoria whispered in barely audible words, "I see our destinies are linked. Our futures are bound together." Blood's passions were so aroused that he chose not to assume the public office to which he had been recently elected. Instead, he abandoned his wife and child in the name of "free love," and took to the road with Victoria, later to marry her in Ohio. Their application for a marriage license—incomplete— remains in the Dayton courthouse records. Though they divorced and remarried and divorced again, Blood remained a reliable friend in the background of Victoria's dramatic public career.

According to Victoria she learned in 1867 that her work was about to begin from Demosthenes, one of her spirit guides and the great orator of ancient Greece. He told her to go to New York City, where a residence would be waiting for her at 17 Great Jones Street. Then he provided her a virtual tour of the house. When Victoria actually arrived in New York with Colonel Blood, Byron, Zula, and Tennie, she found the house just as envisioned, and indeed, it was for rent.

Victoria understood that the first thing she must do was to make money and lots of it. She and Tennie began by selling personal products and remedies to the hundreds of prostitutes in the broth- els around town. These included birth-control sponges soaked in vinegar, scented water, and a clove anesthetic that reduced pain and created warmth. Buck Claflin, sniffing an opportunity all the way from Ohio, tagged along with them, selling opium and his trade- mark "elixir." The sisters' business quickly introduced them to some of the most powerful women among their class in the city, women who "dated" the wealthiest men in the nation.

Perhaps the wealthiest of all the philanderers of New York City was Cornelius "Commodore" Vanderbilt, the steamboat and railroad tycoon, then in his seventies. Vanderbilt was known to be enamored of Spiritualism—and he was lonely. Tennie and Victoria quickly insinuated themselves into his graces as his doting mistress and spiritual guide, respectively. Victoria began by transmitting messages from his long-deceased mother. Soon, Vanderbilt was asking her for stock trading tips. Not that he needed more wealth: He just hated to be bested by his rival tycoons. As it happened, one of those rivals, Jim Fisk, the partner of Jay Gould, was dating Josie Mansfield, an "actress" Victoria knew from the San Francisco days. For a price Josie supplied Victoria with up-to-the-minute information about Fisk's plans to buy and sell. Vanderbilt was getting so much shrewd, timely advice from "the spirits" that he began to pay his medium a percentage of the proceeds.

Victoria clinched her fortune on September 24, 1869, a day known as Black Friday. Fisk and Gould were conniving to corner the market on gold and drive up the price. As soon as Victoria caught wind of this, "the spirits" urged Vanderbilt to sink his fortune into gold at $132 an ounce. Vanderbilt was so giddy with the massive gambit that he promised to share half the proceeds with her. After Thursday's trading, in which the price of gold rose to $144, the spirits counseled selling at $150. Victoria was playing it safe. On the fateful day, Victoria waited in a carriage outside the exchange and watched as the posted price climbed through the 140s and into the 150s. In fact the price reached $164 before President Grant announced his decision to sell treasury gold; by then all the principals in the scam had gotten out. The price plummeted, and most of the small investors were burned.

Victoria's star rose quickly. With her $700,000 profit from the gold sales, she opened a brokerage firm with her sister in downtown New York, breaking into the fraternity of high finance with great aplomb. Of their debut on January 20, 1870, a *New York Herald* reporter wrote: "The general routine of business in Wall Street was somewhat varied today by the mingling in its scenes of two fashionably dressed ladies as speculators. Who they were few seemed to know."

The beautiful sisters from Ohio would not remain nameless for long. Victoria immediately wrote the reporter a note introducing her and her sister; follow-up news stories secured their place on the scene. Long after the other Wall Street offices had shut down for the evening, the offices of Woodhull, Claflin & Co. would be fully lit and abuzz with soiree guests ranging from presidents of large companies to prominent anarchists. The great New Jersey poet Walt Whitman stopped by and proclaimed their endeavor "a prophecy of the future." Tycoons Jay Cook and Jay Gould both placed orders with their firm. Wearing mannish waistcoats and jackets to flaunt their spectacular new freedom, Victoria and Tennie were irresistible—indeed, they were "magnetic."

But becoming the first woman stockbroker was not why Victoria had been sent to New York. Demosthenes visited again: Her real mission was about to commence. Victoria then met Stephen Pearl Andrews, a utopian philosopher advocating equality of the sexes and free love. Andrews saw in her a marvelous vehicle for his ideas, while she heard in his words the very ideas she herself had discovered. The question had always nagged at her: If a woman no longer loved her husband, but stayed married to him and submitted to his sexual demands because she could not support herself, how was she different from the prostitutes Victoria knew, who sold sex and companionship for a living? The answer had primarily to do with social class. The solution as she saw it was for women to claim new public roles—as she herself had done.

In this frame of mind and with Andrews as her inspiration, Victoria declared her candidacy for president of the United States at the end of March. In a paid announcement in the *New York Herald*, she argued that while other women were asking men to change the unjust voting laws, she had acted on her own behalf to change unjust social norms. She concluded, "I therefore claim the right to speak for the unenfranchised women of the country." The election was two years away.

In April 1870 she purchased and furnished a brownstone "palace" in midtown Manhattan, which a dozen or so Ohio Claflins promptly made their home—hastening the inevitable drain on her fortune. In May, with Colonel Blood's editorial help, she began publishing her own newspaper, *Woodhull & Claflin's Weekly*. It printed insiders' political and financial news alongside short stories by George Sand, feminist theory, and, for the first time in America, Karl Marx's entire *Communist Manifesto*, published in Germany in 1848. The paper was eclectic, self-promoting, and charged with intellectual gusto.

The suffragists did not know what to make of this female phenom. Susan B. Anthony, the long-time leader of the movement along with Elizabeth Cady Stanton, had visited the office and was impressed with the boldness with which the women acted and spoke. But Anthony was losing her power in the movement. A new group had arisen that favored a more conciliatory approach to obtaining the vote for women. In the fall of 1870, while these factions continued to hash out their differences, Victoria took a room at the Willard Hotel in Washington, D.C., as a self-appointed lobbyist for the suffrage cause. At issue was a proposal for a sixteenth amendment giving women the vote, which had been stalled in the House Judiciary Committee for over a year. Victoria introduced herself to the members on that committee, including a leading light of Congress at the time, Benjamin Butler of Massachusetts. Butler was lonely—his beloved wife was in Germany, ill with thyroid cancer—and Woodhull offered him solace, companionship, and, it can be inferred, sexual intimacy. As the Sixteenth Amendment seemed destined to die in committee, she and Butler devised a way to recast the legislative debate.

Since its founding *Woodhull & Claflin's Weekly* had argued that the Constitution already guaranteed women the vote. The Fourteenth

Amendment defined citizens as "persons born or naturalized in the United States," with no reference to sex and held that neither Congress nor any state could pass a law abridging the rights due to citizens. In Victoria's eyes the matter simply waited on women's claiming their civil rights. In her weekly she wrote, "I do now proclaim to the women of the United States that they are enfranchised"—that is, possessed of the right to vote.

Butler arranged that she present her views in a memorial to the House Judiciary Committee on January 11, 1871, the very day the suffragists were scheduled to meet in Washington, D.C. In the Congressional chambers that day were Susan B. Anthony and Isabella Beecher Hooker—Harriet Beecher Stowe's younger sister and a leading reformer in her own right—as well as journalists from major New York and Washington newspapers. Not only was this the first time a woman had addressed a Congressional committee, but it was also the first time Victoria had spoken in public. As she began, her voice trembled; then she glanced over at Tennie, also in the audience, and received from her the courage she needed to continue. Perhaps the spirit of Demosthenes also aided her.

Her presentation was magnificent. The suffragists in the audience spirited her to their convention for an immediate repeat performance. Afterward, she was invited to the White House for an audience with President Grant, a fellow Ohioan. He appeared to support her efforts, but did not intervene when the committee voted against adopting her memorial.

Victoria's testimony on the Hill brought her to a new level of fame; her notoriety was yet to come. Now that she had ceased to be just a curiosity and had emerged as a potent force, the attacks on her morals began in earnest. Remarkably, they originated from her own family. The Claflins had always resented Colonel Blood for depriving them of their two best financial assets (never mind that these same characters were living in the Manhattan mansion and blackmailing Cornelius Vanderbilt). In May 1871, as Victoria's fame climaxed in a rousing speech to a suffrage audience, Roxana marched to the justice's office to charge Blood with "corrupting her two daughters" and allowing all kinds of "trash" into their house.

The court case was an extravagant nightmare. There was Roxana's hysterical testimony that communists and free lovers had descended on the house like locusts. There was Tennie's confession: "I have humbugged a great many rich people, I admit it. But I did it to make money to keep all those deadheads." There was the interesting fact that Dr. Canning Woodhull—Victoria's ex-husband—was among those resident deadheads. As Victoria later said, "A thing is only as strong as its weakest link, and that family was the weak link." Following this spectacle, Victoria suffered a furious backlash to her popularity, as suffragists and others scrambled to distance themselves from her.

Victoria strode confidently into battle. Anthony and Stanton had armed her with scandalous facts about the extramarital affairs of Boston and New York's finest—most notably, the liaison between the prominent Brooklyn minister Henry Ward Beecher and Libby Tilton, a parishioner and the wife of his former friend, Theodore Tilton. In her newspaper and in the editorial pages of others, she threatened to hold certain hypocrites to account. How dare they attack her views on free love, when they themselves practiced it! The day her editorials were published, Tilton appeared at her office begging her not to break the scandal, if only for his wife's sake. The tall, handsome Tilton and Woodhull became lovers shortly thereafter. A writer, he composed her biography, which she vainly hoped would bring public understanding and sympathy for "the life of sorrows" she had led. In fact it only worsened Tilton's reputation. The most significant upshot of their three-month affair was Victoria's learning more of the details about the scandalous liaison between Reverend Beecher and his parishioner.

In the meantime *Woodhull & Claflin's Weekly* had become a muckraking organ, committed to exposing fraud anywhere it could be found. There was plenty to expose—the exorbitant salaries of CEOs, taxpayer subsidization of monopolies, and other forms of profiteering—and the *Weekly* was among the first to do so, in exhaustive detail. Added to this detailed picture of systematic injustice were Marxist editorials pointing out, for instance, that Christ and disciples had shared "all things in common." Of course the anti-business themes Victoria was sounding collided head-on with the sisters' own interests: In a campaign speech called "The Impending Revolution," Victoria decried the injustice that allowed a Vanderbilt to lounge in luxury while others toiled for a pittance. Vanderbilt's portrait, hanging on their office wall, had served as the sisters' imprimatur. Alienating him turned their clients away. By mid-1872—election year—the firm had closed.

Family acrimony struck again. In May 1872, as Victoria addressed another suffragist convention, her drugged and drunken sister Utica taunted her several times from the audience. "Are you a free lover?" she demanded to know. "Answer the question."

In exasperation, Victoria shouted, "Yes! I am a free lover! I have an inalienable, constitutional, and natural right to love whom I may, to love for as long or as short a period as I can, to change that love every day if I please!"

In this outburst Victoria and her Equal Rights Party lost the support of virtually all but the Marxists and the die-hard Spiritualists. It was not even certain whether Victoria's running mate, Frederick Douglass, supported her. A newspaper cartoon by the great Thomas Nast pictured her as "Mrs. Satan" with horns. The object of fascination had turned downright ugly in the public's eye.

In this desperate state Victoria revived the *Weekly* for the purpose of publicizing the Beecher affair and vindicating her ideas. The edition sold tremendously, but proved the end for Victoria.

Anthony Comstock, the anti-vice crusader, treated the material as "obscene literature" and had Victoria and Tennie arrested for sending it through the mail—though in fact it was he who arranged to have it mailed. The sisters won their juried court case, a fact the presiding judge outwardly deplored. But Beecher also emerged unscathed through investigations by his own church and a court of law. This, as well as a venomous pamphlet attacking her and her family, convinced Victoria that her mission had foundered. Her radical ideas went through a softening transformation: The "free love" of which she began to speak was "the love of God . . . free to all." After divorcing Blood for good, she moved to England in 1877 with Tennie and her children, so that her daughter, Zula, then "budding into womanhood," would not have to live surrounded by scandal.

In England Victoria married a fifth-generation banker, John Biddulph Martin. Although his family recoiled at the match and refused to attend the wedding, Victoria had cured Martin of sexual impotence, and for that he was eternally grateful. On her part, she became grateful for her husband's "aiding [her] with his wise counsel, that [she might] not stumble." Up to Martin's death in 1897, the two enjoyed a conventional, monogamous marriage: attending various cultural events, traveling to the United States, and sharing an enthusiasm for the new sport of bicycling.

Apart from her marriage Victoria found some comfort in tributes from her more respected colleagues. Elizabeth Cady Stanton and Isabella Hooker visited her in England, gestures that meant the world to her. While it could be argued that Victoria's notoriety set the suffrage campaign back several decades, she had called attention to gender issues of nineteenth-century Victorian society in a way no one would ever forget. In 1892 she visited the United States to run another symbolic campaign for the presidency. At a small but loyal nominating convention, the Equal

Rights Party chose her again as its candidate. This candidacy went largely unnoticed.

What can we make of Victoria—victim and charlatan, entrepreneur and reformer, publisher and politician, visionary, wife, harlot, and mother? This daughter of Ohio was larger than life, like a meteor burning brightly as it enters earth's denser, duller atmosphere. In the end Victoria accepted and loved her life on earth. From 1901 to her death in 1927, she passed her days quietly on a country estate with the company of her sister, son, and daughter. As requested, her ashes were cast "by loving hands" into the sea, to symbolize her everlasting freedom.

HALLIE QUINN BROWN

C. 1854–1949

A Builder of Schools

$\mathcal{H}$allie, at age fifteen, feared she was in over her head. Up to this point, she had received no formal education; now, she sat beside advanced-level students in classes such as Philosophy of History and Biblical Exposition. That was the way it was in the early days of Wilberforce College, when only a few black students could afford college. Though she received some one-on-one tutoring from the school's founder, Bishop Daniel Payne, at whose home she was living, her teachers' questions often left her silent and trembling. She compensated by showing off the physical vigor she had gained doing chores on the family farm in Canada, challenging boys to footraces and often winning them. One day a teacher saw her running and called her to his office: "You have the makings of a fine woman, Miss Brown, if you would give up those ways and apply yourself to your lessons."

According to Hallie, she left his office a changed person. No one had ever called her "Miss Brown" before! She redoubled her efforts and joined the school choir. Later that year, however, when Hallie was called home for a sister's wedding, she found her mother in poor health. Her strong arms and strong back were needed on the farm, so she stayed. She performed her old chores with little enthusiasm, thinking always of Wilberforce. Each night, she knelt beside her bed and prayed, "Oh Lord, please send me back to Wilberforce."

The lineage of Hallie Quinn Brown illustrates the complexity of the family ties of many Southern plantations and the arbitrariness of the relationships that ensued from slavery. Hallie's father, Thomas Brown, was the son of a Scotch woman plantation owner and her common-law husband, who had been a

Hallie Quinn Brown

UNIVERSITY ARCHIVES, CENTRAL STATE UNIVERSITY, WILBERFORCE, OHIO

slave and was the overseer of the property. When she died, he and their children were distributed as slaves among her white relatives; Thomas became the valet of a U.S. Congressman who was his first cousin! Eventually, he bought his own freedom and that of two brothers, a sister, and his aged father. Hallie's mother, Frances Jane Scroggins, was born a slave in Virginia and was freed by her grandfather, a white man. Thomas Brown and Frances Jane Scroggins met and married in Pittsburgh, where they had six children, including Hallie, the fifth, her reputedly auburn hair a throwback, perhaps, to her Scottish grandmother.

The Browns were prosperous, respected citizens of Pittsburgh. Thomas was a steamboat operator on the Ohio and Mississippi Rivers and owned a considerable amount of real estate.

Their three-story, twelve-room house on Hazel Street featured double chandeliers in the dining room and an extra bedroom for "The Bishop," William Paul Quinn, one of the most important men in the history of the African Methodist Episcopal (A.M.E.) Church and a close friend of the family. Thomas was always bringing back stories and surprises from his river trips. On Christmas day the dinner table would be piled high with pheasants, prairie hens, and venison from trades he had made along his Mississippi route.

The Brown home was also a stop on the Underground Railroad. The young children were not privy to the secret comings and goings; they simply wondered why their mother baked so much bread and why it disappeared so fast. Hanging in their home was a photograph of a white family draped in an American flag. Later, the children would learn this family's interesting story. Possessing the "drop" of African blood that destined them for servitude in the South, the people in the picture were runaway slaves who had been tracked from Texas to Pittsburgh by their former masters. After a week of hiding at the Browns', the family finally decided to appear before the arresting officers wrapped in the Stars and Stripes. Incredibly, their protest was successful, and they were allowed their freedom.

This picture, with its multiple paradoxes, seems to comment on the silence surrounding the Browns' removal to Canada in 1864, while the Civil War was still being waged. Hallie gives her mothers' health as the reason for the move, though other factors must have entered in. Perhaps her parents feared post-war reprisals against African Americans or a diminishing of their rights. Perhaps such reprisals had already begun. The war had deflated the value of the Brown properties, so it was not advantageous for them to sell. But sell they did, and moved to a farm outside of Chatham, Ontario, while Thomas continued his work on the riverboats.

Hallie loved her life on the farm, and as she grew older, she became indispensable to its upkeep. She relished the seasonal round of communal activities: corn husking, wood chopping, sleigh rides, sugar camps, quilting bees, and barn dances. And, as her siblings were sickly and her father was often absent, she willingly assumed the bulk of the chores: milking cows, feeding pigs, plucking geese, shearing sheep, planting and cultivating crops, digging potatoes, and pitching hay into the hayloft. Legend has it that this future elocutionist made speeches to the animals she tended, sometimes in their "own" language.

The Pittsburgh transplants brought culture with them, including the first piano of the whole countryside. Next to the Bible on their bookshelf were honored volumes of Shakespeare's plays, Spurgeon's sermons, and a book on Scottish heroes. Still, the Browns could only do so much to educate Hallie. Thomas and Frances themselves had never been to school, nor were there schools in the region for Hallie to attend. One morning when she was fifteen, she heard her father say, "Hallie must be sent away to school, for she will never have a chance here."

One short year later, that memory felt like a dream to Hallie. "Oh Lord, send me back to Wilberforce," she prayed. Finally her prayers were answered. One day, her mother handed her a basket of clean laundry to hang outside and said, "When you get done, I have something to tell you." Frances had devised a plan to send Hallie back to school, rent the farm, and then join her in Wilberforce with her youngest child, Johnny. Thomas Brown approved the plan by mail. Thus, it was the Homewood Cottage, the Browns' new homestead, became a fixture in the village of Wilberforce. So did Frances Jane Brown, known as Ma Brown to the many students who consulted her for advice. And when Thomas retired from his riverboat life, he too settled at Homewood Cottage and became known by the students as Mr. Brown, the Walking Encyclopedia, for his role as a volunteer librarian.

It was at Wilberforce that Hallie began her formal voice training. In 1871 the famous Unitarian minister, author, and philanthropist Edward Everett Hale gave a Commencement Address at which he declared, "What the Negro youth needs to do is to educate his mouth." Hallie did not understand this comment—wasn't her purpose at Wilberforce to educate her mind?—yet she and her classmates responded to Hale's challenge by prevailing upon Bishop Payne to teach the Art of Expression. Hallie had always delighted in reading aloud to Payne, ever since her first months as a Wilberforce student residing in his home; as the youngest girl, she had always been a performer of sorts. She must have relished the opportunity to deliver the salutatory address to her classmates upon graduation from Wilberforce in 1873. She chose for her speech an out-of-the-ordinary topic, "Be Careful How You Make History."

After graduation, imbued with the school's mission of service, Hallie promptly went south for missionary work. She arrived in Yazoo City, Mississippi, and was directed to Sonora, a cotton plantation where former slaves still lived and worked. She was to live in a crude one-room cabin with a couple and their daughter. This she did not mind; however, when she saw the tiny log cabin that would serve as her schoolhouse, her heart sank—"but only for a short time," as she wrote in her unpublished memoir. Still the same sturdy country girl she had been, she enlisted a few strong boys to fell trees; then, with tools borrowed from the Big House, she set to work building a school using carpentry skills she had learned from watching her older brother, Jere. The sight of an educated Northern girl wielding a ripsaw and chisel captured the attention of the folk around the plantation, and this undertaking soon became a community effort. When the structure was finished, there were large chinks between the logs. Hallie and her helpers went to the cotton gin—she on her mule, Sal—and hauled back several sacks of cottonseed to use as a binding agent in the mortar. They repeated the entire process several months later in building a church to replace the shack that had been used for that purpose.

Hallie had a "goodly number" of pupils ranging from eight to sixteen years of age. They came poorly clad, some barefoot, and many used snuff and tobacco (Later, Hallie would hold a bonfire of snuff boxes and corncob pipes.) In addition to teaching reading, writing, and arithmetic, Hallie taught Sunday school and showed the women and girls how to knit and sew. She purchased the supplies for these courses using her own salary and was thrilled when the children arrived to school "tidily dressed." She was sad to leave, eight months later, as she "had become greatly attached to those humble, struggling people."

During the summer, when Hallie was in Wilberforce, she learned of several episodes of unspeakable violence that discouraged her from returning to Mississippi. Years earlier, a pair of Wilberforce graduates, Mr. Patterson and Mr. Ballard, had built a cabin and a school on the Yazoo River, planted corn, cotton, and vegetables, and taught their students how to farm. More recently, Mr. Patterson had run for office in the Mississippi legislature and gotten himself elected. As Hallie wrote, "It was a bitter pill for the rebel element to swallow, this situation of colored men being entrusted with positions of responsibility and honor." The school continued to thrive. But "the mob had set its target." One day, "it swooped down like vengeful vultures and spirits of ill-omen. It demolished the crops, reduced the buildings to ashes and left the lifeless body of young Patterson swaying from a pine tree." Another black man, Mr. Foote, a city tax collector of "sterling character," whom Hallie liked and admired, was beaten to death that year by a mob, on Christmas day. The violent reaction to Reconstruction, exemplified by these events, was to preoccupy the region for many decades to come.

Hallie was next called to a plantation outside Columbia, South Carolina. Here in the wildest reaches of Carolina swampland, she found conditions even worse than those at Sonora, for here reigned over the sharecroppers one Marse Blount, described by Hallie as comparable to Simon Legree in Uncle Tom's Cabin. The end of legal slavery had changed little for Blount's sharecroppers, who were kept in the bondage of their debt to his store, which charged them more for goods, on credit, than they could ever hope to reap from their plots. As Hallie wrote, "They never saw a penny." The sharecroppers could not read or write their names, much less check their accounts at the store. Yet these downtrodden shared with her a trove of folklore so rich that it became the substance of Hallie's dramatic talks later in life.

Hallie admitted that the life she craved was in fashionable, elegant, well-educated society. Yet the day she left the plantation for a new appointment in the city of Columbia, she had a vision in a dream:

"Hundreds of little black children came out of the swamp, their large, sad eyes looking into mine, their small baby hands stretched appealingly to me. Not a word was said, not a sound was heard except the sighing and moaning of a cold wintry wind."

When she awoke, she made a vow that she would "consecrate" the remainder of her life, "while in health and strength, to God and humanity." And indeed, though Hallie left behind the backwoods school buildings and barefoot students, she found a way to use her education to promote their education.

The path to this future led from a two-year tenure as dean of Allen University, an A.M.E. college in Columbia, to Dayton, Ohio, where Hallie taught four years (1882–86) in the public schools. In addition, she petitioned the Dayton Board of Education to open a night school for the adult migrants who were beginning to arrive from the South and taught for four years there as well. Meanwhile, she continued her own education, taking a Chatauqua course on the Art of Speech and Oratory from a Professor Robertson of the Boston School of Oratory. She immediately shared this "mouth training" with her child and adult pupils and began giving lectures and performances as an "elocutionist," or one who performs dramatic readings of other people's texts.

After a brief stint (1892–93) as a dean at Tuskegee Institute, Alabama, the college Booker T. Washington founded in 1891 to train African Americans in the trades, Hallie finally came home to Wilberforce in 1893 as professor of elocution. She did not stay long, however. In 1894 she planned a several-year tour of England—both as tourist and as lecturer and elocutionist. Her primary goal was to represent Wilberforce and raise money on its behalf. Her belief was that the British middle class would be more supportive of efforts to uplift African Americans than was the American middle class. Perhaps this connection had been the plan all along, as the college was named after the British Member of Parliament who had worked to ban the slave trade.

To raise funds for the trip, Hallie lectured her way along the eastern seaboard, with a final date at the Metropolitan A.M.E. Church of New York at the invitation of Frederick Douglass, then at the end of his life. Douglass provided her a letter of introduction to his British friends. This note, however, did not give Hallie the entree into the performing world for which she hoped. For that, some research was needed. In London, her host took her to a show that was billed as "four American women singing Negro melodies." When the curtain lifted, Hallie was flabbergasted to find that the performers, from Georgia, were white. She sat, stunned, through the hour-and-a-half long performance of beloved spirituals such as "Go Down, Moses" and "Swing Low, Sweet Chariot."

In Hallie's words:

> For some time I was too astounded to move or speak. And then I believe I became angry. Here were four southern white girls singing the songs of those whom their ancestors, not too far removed, once held in bondage. The singers were drawing large audiences for such entertainment. While I—well! I went out of that hall with a new determination.
>
> I could sing. I knew every song they had sung. I would sing and I could tell these English people the stories behind my songs. I could depict for them the native settings of each selection—cotton field, auction block slave mart, yes, all. I could further tell of the two hundred and fifty years of bondage and toil without recompense. I could sing. I would sing.

With her renewed determination, she negotiated the terms for her first performance the very next day. And thus, her barnstorming tour began.

Hallie's voice was described as "magnetic." It was compared to that of a mockingbird's because of the variety of tones she could produce. British reviewers ultimately deemed her "one of the finest female elocutionists in the world." This status and the seriousness of her purpose gave her celebrity admission to large gatherings such as the World's Woman's Christian Temperance Congress and the International Women's Congress. She was invited to a garden party hosted by none other than Queen Victoria. In the end Hallie accomplished her purpose. Not only did she raise a sum adequate to significantly expand the Wilberforce campus, but she secured numerous British friends who supported the school's mission. She would return to England and Europe several times for fund-raising.

Back in the United States, Hallie resumed her teaching at Wilberforce. She also became active in the women's club movement, forming a suffrage club, a Woman's Christian Temperance chapter, and a Neighborhood Club. This club work led eventually to membership in the Colored Women's League, later called the National Association of Colored Women (NACW), an organization that supported local African American women's clubs across the nation. From 1920 to 1924 Brown served as president of that organization. In 1924 she spoke at the Republican National Convention in Cleveland.

This black woman who gained entrance into the highest echelons of American, British, and European society could also be a fierce advocate for her people. In 1925 the International Women's Congress was held in Washington, D.C. Despite the inevitable participation of dark-skinned women from other continents, the American organizers decided to segregate African American delegates at the back of the hall apart from the other participants. Hallie spoke out, declaring that unless this policy was changed, all of the African American performers in the musical program would withdraw. The policy was not changed, and as a result of Hallie's speech, black American audience members, as well as performers, boycotted the show.

In her later years, Hallie devoted her efforts to writing. It would have been natural for one who had led such a life to commemorate it in words, but Hallie's scattered memoirs remain unedited and incomplete. She was obviously more interested in producing works that eulogized others; perhaps she felt they would be more immediately helpful to her people and the institution she loved. Between 1924 and 1937 she published five works on

African American legend and folklore, including *Home Spun Heroines and Other Women of Distinction* (1926), a collection of short biographies of noted African American women; and *Pen Pictures of Pioneers of Wilberforce* (1937). Hallie lived a long and productive life of nearly one hundred years. She died in Wilberforce in 1949 and was buried in Massie's Creek Cemetery. Her name still graces the library of Central State University, the technical college that spun off from Wilberforce in 1947. And the old Wilberforce campus where Hallie first "educated her mouth" is now the site of the National Museum of Afro-American History.

ANNIE OAKLEY
1860–1926

Little Sure Shot

$\mathcal{I}$t was the afternoon of Thanksgiving Day 1875. Fifteen-year-old Annie Moses had traveled one hundred miles to spend the holiday with her married sister, Lydia Stein, in Fairmount, a suburb of Cincinnati. Having eaten an early dinner, they were headed northeast in a carriage. Annie's rifle was in her lap.

Francis E. Butler, the performing marksman, had been in Cincinnati for a run at the Coliseum Theater on Vine Street. As usual, he had boasted that he could beat any local who dared to match skills with him in a shooting match. Hotel operator Jack Frost had heard this challenge and thought immediately of the long-haired country girl who supplied his restaurant with fresh game. When he saw Annie that week, he had persuaded her to agree to a contest—though with whom he did not say. Butler was a formidable opponent, among the best in the country.

The match was held in the town of Oakley, just outside Cincinnati. Butler was on the grounds when Annie drove up, wearing a gingham shirtwaist and calf-length skirt she had sewn herself. Butler was not happy to discover that this girl was his opponent and not a member of his audience. No man likes to

MISS ANNIE OAKLEY,
(LITTLE SURE SHOT.)
BUFFALO BILL'S WILD WEST.
ELLIOTT & FRY.   (COPYRIGHT.)   55 & 56, BAKER ST., LONDON, W.

Annie Oakley

compete with a girl: There is no glory in winning—and always the risk of losing. This must have been doubly true of a nineteenth-century man like Butler.

They were shooting live pigeons released from a trap. Fortunately for Annie, Butler went first: Accustomed to hunting in the wild, she had never even seen such a mechanism used before. When Frank said, "Pull," one pigeon was released. He shot it. Annie stepped up, confidently called, "Pull," and shot down her first mark, a dark lively bird. The match was on. The score was tied one to one.

The score was still tied, an incredible twenty-three to twenty-three, in the twenty-fifth and final round. Each shooter had missed one bird and each had one bird left. Popular legend has it that Annie, having proven herself an equal, played the lady and allowed her male opponent to win. But in fact that is not what happened. Perhaps Butler's nerves were strained from the situation. Perhaps he drew a particularly difficult bird. Two things are certain: He tried and he missed. Annie shot her bird and won.

Phoebe Ann Moses was born in August 1860 in a log cabin in northern Darke County, Ohio. She was the fifth daughter of Jacob and Susan Moses, Pennsylvania Quakers who had migrated west just four years earlier. Life on the farm was a never-ending cycle of toil: planting, hoeing, harvesting and canning vegetables, milking the cow, tending the livestock, sewing clothing, and trying to keep their house and persons reasonably clean. The burdens only increased when, after two more children, Jacob died in 1866. Susan then sold the farm and rented a much smaller one, where the family continued the cycle.

Hunger was a frequent visitor to the Moses home. Six-year-old Annie found a way to help. Out in the woods, she dug a pit, stocked it with kernels of corn, and above it wove a trap out of cornstalks and string. This ingenious device captured birds and other small animals for the family's stew pot. Then one day, Annie took down her father's rifle from its resting place above the fireplace mantel. She had watched him closely enough to know how to load the gun and had heard him talk about aiming for the head to keep the animal's flesh uncontaminated with shot. Without her mother knowing, she ventured into the woods and bagged her first game. Shocked, her Quaker mother forbade her access to the firearms.

Within a year the family's financial situation worsened. Susan was forced to send Annie 20 miles south to the Darke County Infirmary in Greenville, a combination orphanage, insane asylum, and nursing home. The director, Nancy Ann Edington, took Annie in to her private abode and taught her to sew and embroider, skills the future performer would use throughout her career. But another, more lucrative offer soon came for Annie's services—from a family she later referred to simply as "the wolves." In addition to boarding her at their homestead south of Greenville, they promised to send her to school. Hungry for an education, Annie agreed. She thus entered two years of brutal servitude. Whether she also suffered sexual abuse is a matter of speculation. She certainly didn't go to school. When she finally found a chance to run away, she had scars on her back and shoulders—and on her psyche, as well. Over the next few years she suffered episodes of near panic that "the wolves" would return for her.

When Annie arrived home, she found that her mother had buried her second husband and married a third, Joseph Shaw, in North Star, Ohio. Neither was in good health. Annie knew she could earn some cash working at the infirmary and so returned. As part of her duties, she sewed school uniforms for the children, adding her own extra finishing touches, and, in Annie's words, "saw to it that each tot had a glass of milk a day." Still, after several harrowing years away, she wanted nothing more than to return to her family—and to the woods and fields she loved so well. With her earnings she purchased a couple of sets of outdoor clothing, copper-toed boots, traps, shot, and powder, and reentered the Shaw household as a young teen, prepared to be a provider.

Annie later joked that, were she to reveal it, her monthly catch in this period might make her seem a "game hog." Of course there was plenty of wild game in those days and no official limits on hunting or trapping. Annie conducted her business with a local merchant, John Katzenberger, who sold her uncontaminated game—Annie always hit her mark—to appreciative restaurateurs in Cincinnati. It was this reputation that led to the Thanksgiving match in Oakley and to a match that would last both parties a lifetime.

It is a rare man who finds his defeat at the hands of a young woman an occasion for wooing. But Butler was a graceful loser. After the awarding of the fifty-dollar prize to Annie, he escorted her to her carriage and gave her and her family free passes to his show. Annie attended and fell in love—with Butler's performing poodle, George, who laid at her feet a tribute: a piece of an apple Frank had shot from his head. Amused, Annie later sent George her greetings. "George" reciprocated with a box of candy to make the wooing official. Butler and Annie were married within the year, but their life together did not begin for several years. While Annie lived out the remainder of her teen years with her mother, Butler was away much of the time, touring as a stage and arena shooter. While home, he tutored Annie in reading and writing, skills the lack of which she felt acutely.

Then, on May 1, 1882, Annie was called to Springfield to take the place of Butler's stage partner, who had fallen ill. Her instructions were simply to hold the objects at which Frank would shoot. Onstage, Annie abandoned this decorous role and insisted on displaying her own talent. Butler, ever gentlemanly, acquiesced, and thus was launched Annie's fabled career as The Rifle Queen and The Peerless Lady Wing-Shot—indeed, as Annie Oakley.

Her assumed name aptly evokes the combined strength, girlishness, and integrity that were her hallmarks. In an age when England's prudish Queen Victoria covered piano legs out of a sense of propriety, Annie too always wore leggings beneath her calf-length skirts. She was 5 feet tall but sturdy, with thick, chestnut brown hair flowing halfway down her back. Her face was less pretty than handsome; and her manner, genuine. She scrupulously avoided the "show-biz" vices of alcohol and tobacco, decorated her tent with flowers, and spent her spare time embroidering. Her customary stage entrance was innocently flirtatious—smiling, skipping, and blowing kisses to the stands. Yet she wielded her weapon deftly and with breathtaking accuracy, and maintained her superb athleticism—and her iron will—even into her sixties.

Butler and Oakley began as a vaudeville act, then joined the Sells Brothers Circus, based in Dublin, Ohio. Traveling with two hippos, a rhino, an elephant, and a giraffe, the circus toured thirteen Midwest states in 1884, finishing at New Orleans the same drizzly November that William Cody's Wild West show was performing there. Buffalo Bill was relatively new to show business himself, but his operation already conveyed his special vision of the Old West—a vision that conferred respect and dignity to Indians and that Mark Twain later declared "wholly free of sham or insincerity." The grounds were clean, and the horses and buffalo impeccably cared for. After visiting Cody's show, Butler and Annie immediately put in an application for hire.

Four long months later, they were granted an audition in Louisville, Kentucky. The audition never occurred: Annie was hired after Cody's partner, Nate Salsbury, observed her practicing her act. Husband Frank now became Annie's assistant, while she became the first white woman to join this mostly male company made up of Indians, Mexicans, and white cowboys—an extraordinarily diverse outfit for the time.

With her honest, open personality, Annie made friends easily. One of her dearest associations that first year was with Sitting Bull, the taciturn Dakota Sioux chief whose lands were among the last of the Indian territories to be taken by force. It was Sitting Bull who reportedly had killed Custer at The Battle of Little Big Horn in 1876, and his movements were increasingly limited by the military authorities. He and Annie had become friends the year before when, on a visit to St. Paul, he had seen her perform with Butler and been touched by her pluck and prowess. He spent the next few days trying to meet her. When she finally relented, he gave her the moccasins he had worn at Little Big Horn and asked to adopt her as his Dakota daughter; when she blithely agreed, he bestowed upon her the Dakota name Watanya Cecilla, or Little Sure Shot.

It was a happy reunion, then, in 1885, when, one month after hiring Annie, Cody won the chief an entire season of freedom by bringing him aboard the Wild West tour. Watanya Cecilla became the tired warrior's closest confidant. In fact he needed her friendship. As he spoke of the broken promises of U.S. authorities, the poverty of his people, and his fears for their future, Annie's compassion must have provided him a way of reconciling with the white race. She wrote to him after that season, but would never see him again.

In fact the entire crew became Annie's family. If she became a daughter to Sitting Bull, she was an older sister to the Cowboy Kid, Johnny Baker, another star shooter. As she had been tutored by Butler, she tutored Baker; on days off, the three would go game hunting together. Cody, whom Annie nicknamed The Colonel, seemed to inspire this sense of group loyalty. When Butler's poodle George died, everyone attended the burial ceremony, and traditional Indian chants accompanied the heart-felt eulogies.

With thoughts of her new show family warming her and Butler through the winter months in North Star, Annie was not prepared for what she faced that spring: Cody had hired a second lady
shooter, one that fit the show biz stereotype in practically every
detail. Boastful, voluptuous, morally loose, and uncultivated in her
manners and speech, not to mention less skilled than Annie, the
Californian Lillian Smith managed to steal some of the limelight
from her clean-cut Ohio rival. Their rivalry drove a wedge between
Annie and The Colonel and poisoned the chemistry of Cody's
show. Annie tolerated Lillian as well as she could through one season and into 1887, when the Wild West show traveled to London
for the season-long Golden Jubilee celebration. There, the two
received equal billing and appeared just one act apart from each
other; as a result, journalists often confused their names and stories. Ironically, when Queen Victoria attended the show and met its
two women performers, she dismissed Annie with the compliment,
"a very clever little girl," while taking time with the immodest Lillian to learn how her gun worked.

Still, Annie Oakley made an indelible impression on her audience. Unlike many stage and arena shooters of the time, she never
relied on trick devices: Her stunts were authentic. She shot clay
pigeons sprung from as many as four traps at a time, using guns in
both hands. Or, she would put her gun down, toss several glass
balls in the air, then dash to retrieve her gun and shoot them all
down. She shot the ash off of Butler's cigarette and a dime out of
his fingers. Most famously, she turned her back to the targets,
perched her rifle over her shoulder, and took aim and fired using a
hand-held mirror.

The latter suggests a symbol for Annie's steady aim concern-
ing her own image as a performer and a Western lady—as opposed
to a Western woman (never mind that she had never been west of
the Mississippi River!). After their stint in London, Annie and

Butler left the Wild West show to try show business on their own. They turned their backs on shoddy outfits and the more compromising vaudeville venues, settling in 1888 for the short-lived Pawnee Bill's Historical Wild West Exhibition and Indian Encampment—a Buffalo Bill clone, but at least one that billed Annie as the World's Champion Woman Rifle Shot. Pawnee Bill's posters went on to boast, "There is but one Annie Oakley—and she is with us." Annie and Frank later found their way back to Cody, but now as independent agents, on their own terms.

Unfortunately, while there may have been only one Annie Oakley, there did exist one Annie Oatley, a nightclub singer. When she died in 1890, the papers carried the news of Annie Oakley's death, convincing many, including her mother, Susan, that Annie was gone for good. That false press was not nearly as shocking as a 1903 wire story filed from Chicago and subsequently published by major newspapers—that a haggard, strung-out Annie Oakley had been caught stealing a black man's trousers to pay for her cocaine habit! Annie was incensed. Apologies and retractions were not enough for her. She sued every major newspaper that carried the story. While some people questioned her motives, Annie was clear on the matter: Only by drawing this kind of attention to the mistake could she hope to rectify it utterly in the public's mind. Over the next six years, many of her days were spent in courtrooms and lawyers' offices. The educated speech and manners she had struggled to cultivate now helped her cause, as she testified from the stand in well-constructed sentences, wearing tailored outfits that bespoke her seriousness. In the end Annie was vindicated, winning all her cases.

Money was not the issue in these cases for Annie. Nor was her personal reputation the sole issue. She saw beyond her image to what her image had become. Annie was a standard-bearer of the healthful and wholesome expansion of women's activities outside the home. As such, she had sternly fought attempts to stereotype such initiatives and the women who took them as somehow fast or loose. The 1890s had seen an expansion of the accepted sphere of women. So-called Gibson Girls sported shorter, mid-calf skirts and bloomers, in part to free them to ride the new-fangled bicycles. While Annie preferred leggings and always rode sidesaddle on her horse, she also embraced the bicycle craze and devised her own cycling costume: Beneath her skirt she wore both gaiters, or laced leggings, and knickerbockers—trousers gathered at the knee. While in London, Annie offered private shooting lessons to English ladies of the landed class, known for its love of the hunt. Her appearance at gun clubs in the eastern U.S. helped open the membership of those clubs to middle-class American women as well.

It could be said that Annie appeared at the right time and place for the talent she had to offer. In 1890 historian Frederick Jackson Turner famously declared that America's western frontier was closed; this realization only whetted people's appetite for visions of the Old West. But everyone who met Annie declared it was not her image but her authentic personality that made her shine so brightly. None other than Will Rogers determined that "she was a greater character than she was a rifle shot." After performances her tent would be crammed with gifts of flowers, books, and other tributes. She received dozens of medals and special pieces of jewelry from dignitaries, along with numerous invitations, even marriage proposals, from complete strangers. All this attention did not turn her head. She knew she was not from the West, but from the log cabin home of an Ohio Quaker family. No matter how accustomed she became to finery, when she visited her mother's North Star home, her self-appointed jobs were to shoot and pluck the family's supper and to clear the farm of snakes. In fact she looked forward each year to performing these chores. While on tour, she sought out poor children and widows who could use cash assistance. In addition she helped as many as twenty women obtain schooling. She organized shows to benefit orphanages, and when the Wild West show came to Cincinnati in her final year of performing, 1913, she bought tickets for all the inmates of the Darke County Infirmary.

Annie had caught a glimpse of her mortality while riding a train north from Charlotte, North Carolina, to Virginia in 1901. She was traveling with the Buffalo Bill troupe when a passing train plowed into them. As many as 120 horses were injured and had to be shot. Annie, thrown from her seat, incurred only a minor head and back injury, but when she emerged from the hospital, her hair had turned stark white. Annie continued to perform, wearing a dark-colored wig. Twenty-one years later, in 1922, she found herself trapped under a Cadillac in Leesburg, Virginia, with a fractured hip. Worse, their beloved dog, Dave, chose that month to die. Finally accepting their retirement, Annie and Butler settled in Dayton to be near family and even adopted a new dog, Dave II. Annie divided up her mementoes among various relatives and sent clippings of Dave's obituary, which summarized their recent history, to all who inquired about her. Finally, on November 3, 1926, she passed away. Butler stopped eating and followed her in death eighteen days later. They were buried together in a cemetery near Greenville—on Thanksgiving, the very day they had met fifty-one years earlier.

HELEN HERRON TAFT
1861–1943

White House Bound

Sharp, cracking sounds came from the bluish windows. Rising from bed, Nellie saw ice-coated trees thrashing in the wind, black, broken limbs and twigs scattered across the snowy White House lawn. The sight might have been sublime, had this not been the day for which she had waited her entire adult life. Today, March 4, 1909, her husband, William Howard Taft, would become president of the United States. She could just envision the inaugural procession skidding out of control into a ditch.

Later that morning, Taft would comment, "I always said it would be a cold day when I got to be president of the United States." He had wished all his life to avoid this day—but knew he could not, not while married to Nellie.

Mr. and Mrs. Taft had been overnight guests of the outgoing president, a change in precedent intended to symbolize the friendship of the two men—the bellicose Theodore Roosevelt and his affable, gigantean secretary of war. Edith Roosevelt and Helen did not share such a friendship, a fact that had made their dinner the night before a bit awkward. And, sadly, the storm was a better portent of how the men's friendship would develop. The two men left

Helen "Nellie" Herron Taft

early for the Capitol so that Roosevelt might sign a few bills before handing over power. Roosevelt said his last goodbye to the White House; he did not intend to ride back with his successor as other outgoing presidents had done.

In the hours between Will's departure and her own, Nellie fretted over her appearance. According to the newspapers, she wore "a purple satin suit and a hat trimmed with gold lace and a high white aigret." With her typical, self-deprecating wit, she remarks in her memoirs, "This is as good a description as any, though it might have been more flattering, considering the importance I attached to the subject." She had struggled with the egret plume the day before, when it was singed by a lighted gas jet, and felt self-conscious about its resultant droop.

The new president delivered his inaugural address inside the Senate Chamber. As soon as he finished, Nellie hurried from the gallery so that she might intercept him in the rotunda before he made his way outside. If Teddy Roosevelt was not going to ride with her husband in the inaugural parade, then she would! She would be the first woman to do so! With a few words she fended off objections from officials, then lightly took her place next to her beaming husband in the open coach. The sun now shone overhead. It ricocheted against the ice and snow, bedazzling Nellie's senses. Yes, this was what she had waited for. The cheers of the crowds along Pennsylvania Avenue seemed to multiply, too, as Nellie felt the "secret elation" reserved for those who are conscious of making history.

After the parade Nellie explored her new home, imagining how she would manage the vast premises—what rooms she would use for what occasions, what furnishings she would place where. With not a minute to spare, she rushed to her room, finding both her hairdresser and costume waiting. The gown had been embroidered in Tokyo; its silver threads glittered against the heavy white satin. That morning, it still had not arrived from the New York dressmaker, its progress held up by the ice. After three unfortunate attempts by the hairdresser to perfect her coiffure, Nellie resigned herself once more to imperfection, dressed herself in her new gown, and descended to the car waiting to whisk her and America's twenty-seventh president off to the inaugural ball.

Helen Herron was born in Cincinnati in 1861. Her mother was the daughter of a U. S. congressman from New York. Her father, an attorney, was a college roommate of President Benjamin Harrison at Miami University and a former law partner of President Rutherford B. Hayes. Put simply, the family was well connected with Ohio's political aristocracy, which flourished in the national arena after the Civil War. Hayes's ascension to the presidency in 1877 prompted numerous visits by the Herron family to the White House, one to christen the latest Herron arrival Lucy Hayes Herron. To her "intense excitement" Nellie was specifically invited for a two-week stay in the White House with her newlywed sister Jennie and her husband. There, in the serene but welcoming environment presided over by the popular Lucy Hayes, seventeen-year-old Nellie daydreamed about how she herself might set the tone if she were first lady.

Nellie was more highly strung than Lucy Hayes, however. As an adolescent, she was consumed by the study of music and shed tears when she felt her talent did not justify continuing. Her diary reveals a young woman impatient with her debutante life, wishing rather that she could write a literary work or have a career. She craved the opportunity to prove herself. She was petite, but lacked distinctive beauty, and doubted that any man would be drawn to her. Nellie did have a quick, ironic wit and a cultivated mind, and these features were highlighted by the social life she and her friends pursued. She never missed a musical event and organized games of charades and even full-fledged dramatic productions. In one burlesque, her future husband played the title role in "Sleeping Beauty."

Will and Nellie first met at a small sledding party near the Taft house in Mt. Auburn when she was eighteen. A recent graduate of Yale, he had returned to Cincinnati to study and practice law. It was several years later that he regularly began to appear at the Herron residence, conveniently located on Pike Street, just steps away from the home of his older brother, Charles. Perhaps to further the intimacy, Nellie in 1883 organized a Saturday night "salon" at her house—an "invitation-only" study and discussion group—with Will, his brother, Horace, her sister, Maria, and herself at the core. Will was indeed impressed by his hostess, who had been known to read German literature while drying the dishes, and humbly submitted to her tutelage in all things literary and cultural. Gradually, he parleyed the role of pupil into that of suitor. But Nellie's moods were a mystery. She accepted his marriage proposal but refused to make it public, then reduced Will to—in his sister-in-law's words—a "mountain of misery" during the long year of their engagement with her cold responses to his lovesick letters.

Finally, a date in June 1886 was set. Nellie's father bought property for them in Walnut Hills overlooking the Ohio River, and they spent the winter months designing their ideal home. In the spring Nellie shopped for her dress in Washington, where Will wrote her, "I wonder, Nellie dear, if you and I will ever be there in any official capacity," adding the quip, "Oh yes, I forgot, of course we shall when you become Secretary of the Treasury."

For all her fine taste, Nellie was known to be frugal. On June 19 a large crowd gathered in the Herron home for the wedding ceremony, as was customary. After attending to the final instructions for the house construction, Nell and Will sailed to Europe for an extended honeymoon. Nellie later boasted that they enjoyed themselves on only $5 a day.

Within a year Will had been appointed to fill a vacancy on the Superior Court of Ohio, then ran and was elected to that position in the general election. He was never happier; he loved the law and excelled at being a judge. Nellie, however, was not so pleased. Her husband "seemed to suddenly take on a maturity and sedateness quite out of keeping with his actual years." She feared that he—and she—would miss out on life's dramas if he pursued a career in the judiciary and preferred for him a more diverse experience.

Nellie got her wish in 1890 when President Benjamin Harrison appointed her husband to be solicitor general, the lawyer for the federal government in cases before the Supreme Court. Such a role, she felt, would allow Will to develop and exercise "initiative and originality." It also meant residence in Washington for her and her newborn son, Robert. While interesting at first, her life settled into quiet routine, and another child, Helen, was born. As she wrote in 1914, Washington in the early 1890s had not yet become a "brilliant social center" where "large dinner parties, balls, receptions, musicals and other entertainments [were] of daily and nightly occurrence."

The Tafts returned to their Ohio home in 1892 when Will was appointed to the Sixth Circuit Court of Appeals, the Cincinnati-based federal appeals court for Ohio and three surrounding states. During the eight years he served as a circuit judge, Nellie found her own projects to pursue in her hometown. Chief among these was the Cincinnati Orchestra Association Company, which she founded in 1895 in order to create a city orchestra. That first season, she and fifteen other women raised funds for nine concerts at Pike's Opera House. In the next several years, the orchestra grew in both size and importance, hosting Richard Strauss as a guest conductor and premiering Gustav Mahler's great Symphony No. 5. At last, Nellie had found a way to express her own cultural interests and talents.

The next chapter in the Tafts' lives introduced an entirely new cultural adventure. Under President McKinley, the United States intervened to support neighboring Cuba in its war for independence from Spain. As the Spanish-American War developed, the Philippines, another Spanish colony seeking independence, came into play. In the 1898 Treaty of Paris, which ended the war, the United States gained authority over this vast and distant archipelago. One year later, William Taft received a telegram from McKinley requesting that he come to Washington immediately. The president wanted to ask him in person to head a U.S. commission to establish civil government in the Philippines, where armed resistance to U.S. military occupation was still strong. Not because he approved of American imperialism, but because the goal was to make the Philippines self-governing, Taft agreed.

Nellie was thrilled and immediately read all the available books on the region. Her sister Maria agreed to come along. A number of the other commissioners and their wives decided not to bring their children for fear of deadly tropical diseases, but Nellie focused on the cultural benefits that her children—now three in number—would gain from life in a foreign country. In Japan a sore throat forced Charlie, Nellie's two-year-old son, into quarantine for diphtheria; just as he recovered, Robert fell ill with the same symptoms. Nellie joined each in quarantine, while the commissioners traveled on to the Philippines. Finally, Nellie and her children joined Will in Manila, safely crossing the China Sea in the middle of the typhoon season. Nellie writes about these challenges in her memoirs as if they were only slight drawbacks to the grand learning adventure that a foreign country offered.

After centuries of harsh Spanish rule and one year of occupation by the authoritarian U. S. general Arthur MacArthur, the expansive, smiling William Howard Taft confounded the Filipinos with his open-mindedness and geniality. On their tour of the islands, the Tafts acted more like diplomats than the leaders of an occupying force. One reason was their progressive thinking about culture and race. While Nellie found a few of the Filipinos' customs exasperating, she did not—as colonialists did—brand her darker-skinned brothers and sisters as inferior. In her words, "We insisted upon complete racial equality for the Filipinos."

She reveals this open-minded perspective in her observations of the "non-Christian" mountain people in northern Luzon. Soon after she and Will returned from their island tour, she and Maria were invited on a two-week horseback inspection trip of the tribes by a U. S. general and his wife. Nellie—no outdoorswoman—"looked with considerable trepidation to the prospect of a long and necessarily intimate association with a horse," but was nonetheless excited to go on what promised to be a highly educational, if somewhat dangerous, journey across difficult terrain. Will encouraged her to go, though according to her, "I should probably have gone without this advice." The tribesmen of these mountains were "as unlike Filipinos as American Indians are unlike Englishmen." In custom they were "to all intents and purposes . . . naked savages." Yet, she writes, "it is these same incomprehensible 'naked savages' who have built the thousands of acres of rice terraces which are a marvel and a mystery to every irrigation expert or technical engineer who has ever seen them."

Perhaps the feature of Filipino culture that most delighted Nellie was the Luneta, an oval-shaped track with bandstands on either end. Every evening, the Luneta was the place to promenade, to see and be seen, to listen to music and enjoy oneself in the company of society at large. When Nellie became America's First Lady, one of the first things she did was to create a "luneta" out of West Potomac Park in Washington, complete with a bandstand and a circular drive.

With Taft's official appointment as governor of the Philippines in 1901, Nellie made her own impact on the social scene there. She returned from her sojourn in Luzon to find that her husband had invited 2,000 guests to the inaugural reception, far more than their house could hold. Then, just before the party, "the heavens opened and . . . a sheet of water descended," forcing the festivities inside. In her typically buoyant fashion, she wrote, "It was a crush, and a warm crush, but it was a gala occasion, everybody was in good humor." Once installed in the governor's palace, Nellie held garden parties open to all regardless of race or class. Indeed, she made it her personal goal for these gatherings to be racially mixed. As she states in her memoir:

> The Filipinos had to have a little coaxing before they began to avail themselves very freely of our general invitation. But by asking many of them personally and persistently to 'be sure and come Wednesday' we prevailed on a good number to believe they were really wanted; and after a little while there began to be as many brown faces as white among our guests.

Such gestures went far to inculcate in Filipinos the principles of democracy—the very purpose of the commission's presence there. As her husband's closest adviser, Nellie knew that the little things mattered: "Even in our daily round of social affairs we dealt with tremendous problems whose correct solution meant the restoration of peace and prosperity." Thus, she continued these parties, even during a deadly cholera epidemic, to rally people's spirits and maintain good relations with the islanders.

William Howard Taft's name had been mentioned in 1900 for a Supreme Court vacancy, a prospect that Nellie rejected outright, despite her husband's keen interest in the job. His name arose again in 1904, under President Theodore Roosevelt, who had assumed office after President McKinley's 1901 assassination. This time, Taft himself objected: While the Philippines were making great strides toward self-government, he felt his work there was incomplete. Later that year, however, Roosevelt asked Taft to be his secretary of war. The situation in the Philippines had progressed positively, and with Nellie's blessing, the family left their tropical palace forever. They were missed: The Taft years in the Philippines are generally considered a high-water mark in colonial administration by any country.

The new role provided Nellie more opportunities to travel—for instance to accompany her husband to Panama for the opening of the canal. It also drew her into the corridors of power. When Roosevelt won the presidential election in 1904, he announced that he would not run in 1908. To Nellie, this meant that her husband could become the next Republican nominee, especially if Roosevelt would back him. However, another seat opened on the Supreme Court in 1906, and William Howard Taft was first on the list, again. Knowing his wife's views, Taft hesitated. After meeting separately with Nellie, the president told Taft that he understood his friend's reluctance to cross her and looked for another appointee.

Still, Roosevelt resisted Nellie's request that he immediately throw his support behind her husband and chided her for being too ambitious on her husband's behalf. For her part Nellie distrusted Roosevelt's motivations—after all, she wondered, why would anyone give up the *presidency?*—and a subtle acrimony took hold and began to fester. It would be present in the tense relations between the outgoing and ingoing first ladies, that stormy March evening in the White House. But it would not become full blown until Taft reversed some of Roosevelt's policies as president. By the next election cycle, the feud would tear the Republican Party into two factions, with Roosevelt running his famous Bull Moose third party campaign, and would result in a Democrat—Woodrow Wilson—winning the White House.

Lacking Roosevelt's early endorsement for her husband's candidacy, Nellie began contacting other Republican brass for support. From early 1907 through the election in 1908, Nellie managed the campaign of her reluctant candidate, revising speeches, monitoring newspaper coverage, and maintaining constant contact with Republican power brokers. His nomination and election to the presidency were her personal triumph. It is bitterly ironic, then, that one month after they moved into the White House, after she had redecorated the manse with her Far Eastern tapestries and furniture, she suffered a stroke that temporarily paralyzed her right side and left her unable to speak. One can picture her taking her meals—as she did—behind a screen outside the State Dining Room, trying to overhear the political discussions inside. Or attending Cabinet meetings, stoic in her silence. But the story takes on an even deeper pathos when one considers the role her husband played. Through the long months of his first year in office, he waited on her faithfully, spending hours each day helping her regain her speech. In fact he needed her; she was his closest adviser.

William Howard Taft is generally considered a failed president. His redemption came in 1921 when he finally joined the Supreme Court. In fact he was appointed chief justice by the last of the Ohio presidents, Warren G. Harding, and performed admirably, as everyone knew he would. Nellie Taft, however, is considered a notable first lady. Not only did she achieve several "firsts" in this capacity, but she participated as a full partner in her husband's political decision making. She also threw lavish garden parties—on a tight budget—and was responsible for planting the Japanese cherry trees that bloom so famously every spring in Washington. Her greatest moment in the White House was the nighttime celebration on the White House lawn of her and her husband's 1911 silver wedding anniversary. The trees were lit with a myriad of lights, with lanterns strung between them, and 5,000 guests thronged the reception line. Upon leaving the White House, she began another tradition by donating her silver-embroidered inaugural gown to the Smithsonian Institution, now part of the ever-popular first ladies exhibit.

Nellie was hurt by the result of the 1912 election, as was her husband. But as she wrote, "Fortunately we are a family that laughs." The Taft family was also a family of great talent and drive. Of the three children, Robert became a U.S. senator and a Republican nominee for president in his own right; Helen, a dean of Bryn Mawr College; and Charles, the mayor of Cincinnati. A grandchild also became a senator, and a great-grandchild, the governor of Ohio. Nellie's memoirs display both aspects of the family character: the lively humor and the rigorous intellectual grasp of the world. Though her willful reign over her husband is easily caricatured and her role as Washington hostess a fabled one, her story is far more complex and interesting. Her cultural achievement in founding the Cincinnati symphony orchestra and the enlightened intelligence with which she and her husband governed the Philippines at a time when colonial relations around the world were rife with racism and a full decade before the United States would elect its last openly racist president, Woodrow Wilson—these hallmarks of her life should not be forgotten.

Nellie outlived Will, who died in 1930. She remained interested in national affairs until her death in 1943. She was buried in Arlington National Cemetery, the first presidential wife to receive this honor.

JANE EDNA HUNTER
1882–1971

A Beacon for the Black
Working Woman

$\mathcal{J}$ane Edna Hunter came to Cleveland on a whim. At age twenty-three she had just completed her training as a nurse at the Hampton Institute in Virginia. On her way to Florida to find a job, she'd stopped in Richmond to visit her Uncle Parris. His friends, Mr. and Mrs. William Coleman, were moving to Cleveland and in their excitement talked Jane into joining them. Thus, in 1905 Jane became part of the first wave of the Great Migration, the northward move of African Americans to industrial cities like Chicago, Cleveland, and Detroit. In years to come, millions more would come.

Deboarding the train, Jane and the Colemans struck out to find a place to stay the night. At the first place Jane knocked, the man who answered looked her over with a keen eye, and then noticed the Colemans standing behind her. "Lady, I don't think this is the place you want," he said, closing the door in her face. Jane later realized that she had called on a house of prostitution. The three eventually found a rooming house on Central Avenue.

Jane Edna Hunter

Jane's initial complaint was that it was overpriced. After paying a week's rent in advance, she had money for only two meals. She advertised immediately as a nurse skilled in massage, giving her new address. The responses she received insinuated something she did not at all intend. The details began to fall into place. The landlady's daughter, Velma, wore flashy pink undergarments and stayed out until early morning. The landlady drank alcohol and pushed it on her. These people were not like the folks among whom Jane had been raised.

One evening Jane accepted a friend's invitation to go dancing at Woodluff Hall. The sights inside astonished her—women wearing heavy makeup and short skirts; men swaggering about, half-intoxicated. A nicely dressed man introduced himself and asked her to dance. He was curious about her origins. She explained that she had just moved to the city and was looking for work as a nurse. "Little girl," he said, with a stern paternal air, "You're in the wrong church and the wrong pew. This is not the place for nice girls like you."

The city, it turned out, was a dangerous place for girls who did not yet have their bearings. Jane was lucky; many other girls found themselves victims of the vice lords who found fresh recruits for their enterprises in places such as the ones upon which Jane had stumbled. In fact the owner of Woodluff Hall was one Starlight, an underworld figure whose rise to power in Cleveland would parallel Jane's own rise to prominence. Jane moved to a safer neighborhood, but never forgot what she had learned and what it almost cost her to learn it. Soon enough, she would put this "education" to good use.

Jane Edna Harris was born in 1882 in Pendleton, South Carolina, the oldest daughter of Edward and Harriet Harris, hard-working sharecroppers struggling to make a decent life for their family. Her father was light-skinned, the child of a plantation overseer and a slave; his thoughts and actions, according to Jane, were ruled by "English blood." By contrast her mother was dark-skinned and uneducated, one of nineteen children. Jane herself was the lightest hued of her siblings and was named for her father's English grandmother. She identified with her father's ardent wish that his children be educated; her mother had no such wish. In her parents' ongoing clashes, mostly caused by Edward's violent bouts of jealousy, little Jane was loyal to him and even justified his violence as due to his white ancestry. Her childhood "aversion" to her stubborn, enduring mother—and implicitly to her "African blood"—would trouble her deeply as an adult.

Childhood in the country held its inevitable delights: Jane loved to hunt frogs in the streams and was at once horrified and thrilled by her occasional encounters with water moccasins. Her mother's parents, the Milliners, had their own farm nearby; Jane could always run down the dirt road to Grandma Milliner's for biscuits and jam or fresh milk from Reddy the cow. When she and her brother grew older, Edward Harris quit farming and moved to town so they could attend the nearby school. In the fall, Jane picked cotton alongside adults, joining in the spirituals they sang to lighten their heavy loads.

At age ten Jane's childhood came to an abrupt end with the death of her father, her "truest friend." Harriet Harris became the live-in cook of a Clemson family, where no children could follow her. Jane was sent to live with an aunt and from there to Anderson, South Carolina, to work as a maid for a family that exploited her. At age twelve she began working as a waitress and maid in a hotel where she was subject to constant sexual harassment, until another aunt rescued her and brought her back to Pendleton and the cotton fields. Then, when she was fourteen, a traveling black missionary couple, Rev. and Mrs. E. W. Williams, noticed her "earnestness and desire to please" and offered her a work-study arrangement at their boarding school. With her mother's reluctant blessing, Jane attended the school for four years, gaining a basic education in English, math, history, and speech. Moreover, after starting with menial household tasks, she worked her way up to dining room manager and fund-raising intern for the school. In 1900 at age eighteen she was the school's star graduate.

Jane liked to tell one incident from those years that expressed the vision that motivated her later work. After spending the summer in Pendleton, she had not earned enough money to buy her train ticket back to school, located 45 miles away. A friend had promised to buy her ticket, but was nowhere in sight when the train arrived. In response to her distress, the group of neighbors who had gathered to bid her off—themselves quite destitute—pooled what little change they had to buy her the ticket. Ten years later, Jane would ask her Cleveland friends to pool their nickels for a mutual aid fund for African American girls.

After graduating from the Williamses' school, Jane no longer fit in at Pendleton. Her aunt's house was crowded. She and her sisters were essentially homeless. Having had a taste of education, she wanted more. As she worked in the fields and sang the spirituals, new sorrows were released. She had found true love, but her mother stood in its way, for reasons Jane does not divulge in her autobiography. Defeated, she and her sweetheart went opposite ways: He married an older woman whom he did not love, and Jane married an older man, Edward Hunter, whom she did not love. Unsurprisingly, this loveless marriage added nothing of significance to her life. After fifteen months she announced to Mr. Hunter that she was leaving for Charleston to work. He agreed without asking for details. The marriage was unofficially over.

Jane's wages as a skilled domestic worker in Charleston enabled her to send her sisters to the Williamses' boarding school. Shortly thereafter, an influential black woman, Mrs. Ella Hunt, persuaded her to train to be a nurse. In Jane's words, "I studied indefatigably, mastering the names of a hundred instruments, keeping eyes and ears alert all times to the needs of the operating surgeon." Through such efforts, she earned a good reputation and enjoyed a variety of appointments, both among the wealthy and the poor. Of the latter, she wrote, "Work in the horrible slums of historic Charleston was no less a privilege than the experience in the homes of the well-to-do." The conditions she witnessed activated her desire to do something useful for her race. After a brief advanced course at the Hampton Institute, a school that promoted "racial uplift," Jane was ready to try her profession someplace new.

Jane's initial attempts to find work as a nurse in Cleveland were discouraging. To her surprise, she "met rebuffs" that, in her words, "seemed much more severe" than those she'd encountered in Charleston. Jane had assumed that the North would present plenty of opportunities for black personal nurses, but white Northerners were unaccustomed to that sort of interracial intimacy. More ominously, racial attitudes in Cleveland and other Northern industrial cities were undergoing dramatic change. In the nineteenth century, Cleveland had accepted blacks into skilled trades and even elected black legislators. African Americans owned their own houses throughout the city, side by side with whites. As the new century dawned and the newcomers began to arrive from the South, blacks were increasingly barred from white neighborhoods and white-collar jobs. The new migrants were even barred from the settlement houses that had been established to help immigrants adjust to American society. Just as Jane had discovered, there was no place for the newcomers from the South to stay.

By 1909 Jane had finally found a home to share with a friend in a quiet neighborhood of East Cleveland. Moreover, her income from nursing assignments and other odd jobs enabled her to purchase a parcel of land back home in Pendleton. After years of internal struggle, she was ready to forgive her mother for being who she was—which was, after all, a generous, hardworking, morally upright woman. Jane planned to build a home for her mother on the land she had bought, but her plans were destroyed by her mother's unexpected death. This threw Jane into a depression so severe that she put aside her efforts to advance her nursing career. She had failed to reconcile with her mother. Would she fail to reconcile with her race? As she emerged from a yearlong descent into remorse, she began to ask the question, "How can I give to the world what I have failed to give her?"

She was still asking herself this question one August day in 1911 when she encountered a young black mother of twins whom she was helping return to Alabama. Shamed by her family, "Ruth" had run away to Cleveland with her babies. Unfortunately, she had no domestic skills and no one would hire her. Jane had interceded, writing the family a letter and offering to pay her train fare home. But this day, the regret she felt for "Ruth" seemed connected to the regret she felt for her mother. There should be, she realized, a place in Cleveland for women like "Ruth," a place where an African American girl could live cleanly and learn skills to help her get a decent start in the city. Since the YWCA as well as the settlement houses barred black women, her people needed their own "settlement house."

Jane introduced the idea to some friends, and together they formed the Working Girls' Home Association, with dues of a nickel apiece. The club spread rapidly through the black churches. Obviously, the nominal dues allowed for a wide membership base, but not for the funds Jane would need to purchase, equip, staff, and operate the facility she envisaged. She would have to depend on wealthy whites for the bulk of her funding. Five years of nursing work had brought her in contact with some such potential donors, and she built on those connections. In speaking with them, she emphasized the role her facility would play in supplying trained domestic help to white homes. To attract more money, she agreed to a white-dominated board of directors. While established blacks disliked the idea of segregated facilities and activist blacks resented the control by whites of their institution, Jane's Southern approach, combining segregation and paternalism, proved the most effective at that time. In 1913 the Phillis Wheatley Association—a name chosen by Jane to honor the black poet from Boston—opened a home near the corner of 40th Street and Central Avenue, in the heart of what was rapidly becoming the black section of the city.

Jane's dream had become reality at just the right time. From 1910 to 1920 the black population in Cleveland tripled from a huge influx of Southern blacks, earning the city the nickname of Alabama North. At the same time, the nation's tone grew increasingly racist. As President Woodrow Wilson segregated government and implicitly condoned the 1916 rebirth of the Ku Klux Klan, blacks in Cleveland were excluded from all neighborhoods except for the Central Area. Rents in this section were inordinately high, simply because demand was so great. Each wave of migration from the South funneled more bodies into the already crowded neighborhoods. Families doubled up, apartments deteriorated, and landlords simply charged more, in a vicious cycle that bred crime and despair. In Cleveland and other cities, the modern slum was being born.

Vice was profitable for some, however, and Starlight, whose real name was Albert D. Boyd, was determined to keep it so. This brothel owner was sufficiently cozy with the Republican bosses to name his own city council candidate to represent the Central Area ward. In 1910 Thomas Fleming became the first black elected to the city council of a major American city, but he quickly became a liability to Cleveland's black population when he was appointed to oversee the police department. With Fleming as his tool, Starlight could conduct his business at will. Only the pawns of his business—the unfortunate young women—faced arrest. Jane campaigned furiously to oust Fleming from office. Her candidates lost repeatedly in elections that were probably rigged. In one confrontation with Starlight, she shook her finger in his face, saying, "Someday I'll get you, you rascal." After all she and Starlight were in a pitched battle over the futures of the young working women who stayed at the Phillis Wheatley.

The courses offered by the Phillis Wheatley Association focused mainly on training for domestic work—cooking, laundry, and dining room service—the skills Jane had mastered at the Williamses' missionary school. The association's philosophy was squarely in line with that of Booker T. Washington, The Great Accommodator, who, as the president of Tuskegee Institute, a technical college for African Americans, also found himself asking wealthy white donors for funds. He claimed that the best way for African Americans to advance was to improve their economic skills and character; eventually whites would recognize their black brothers' equal humanity and capabilities. Jane accommodated both racist and sexist ideologies as to the proper sphere of black women's work. The PWA served as an employment agency for the girls it had trained, yet it set no standards for employers such as a minimum wage or maximum-hour workday; doing so might have offended its donors. In many cases, the women were exploited. Jane excused such situations with the philosophy that such trials helped build the women's character.

The home soon needed larger quarters, as increasing numbers of women and girls opted for its safe shelter. Jane was confident of her abilities to raise the needed money from her white "friends"— and rightly so. In 1918 the PWA bought and renovated a seventy-two-room apartment building, and in the following year an adjacent two-story building was purchased for activities. In 1922

Jane began another fund-raising campaign that, with a sizable contribution from John D. Rockefeller Jr., resulted in the completion, in 1926, of a new eleven-story building on Cedar Avenue—the largest such facility in the nation.

While her fund-raising prowess was undeniable, Jane was insecure, both about the status of the PWA as an independent institution and about her own qualifications to be its leader. Many of the Northern-trained blacks on the PWA staff had high school and even college educations; in the South Jane had received the equivalent of an eighth-grade education with additional technical training. Moreover, she wanted to learn more about managing money. Thus, in 1922 she began studying law at Cleveland's Baldwin Wallace College. She passed the Ohio bar examination in 1926—the same year that the grand, new Phillis Wheatley building was completed.

Since its founding the Phillis Wheatley Association had strived to be a social gathering place as well as a shelter and training center. After all, part of the battle for good character was to light the way toward healthy forms of recreation. From the very first its dining room was popular among Cleveland's established blacks as well as newcomers, and was one of the only freely integrated restaurants in the city. This aspect of the association's mission was enhanced by the Depression, when other forms of recreation became either illegal or simply too expensive to pursue. There were lectures in "Negro history," music lessons of all kinds, and drama, basketball, tennis, and dancing clubs. In addition it offered day care and hosted "camps" for children.

The cataclysm of World War II taught Americans the evils of racial supremacist thinking, and by the time it ended, things had begun to change. The Cleveland YWCA began accepting blacks. The city formed a committee to examine cases of discrimination within municipal employment. Still more blacks migrated to the region, and for the first time, black businesses were founded to serve the community. The methods of the Phillis Wheatley Association, anchored as they were in turn-of-the-century race relations, had become outmoded. Jane's beliefs were themselves outmoded. The racial bias of her youth, which she had never truly escaped, was now anathema to the progressive element of society, to which programs such as hers rightly belonged. In 1947, as Jane turned sixty-five, the board voted for her "retirement."

Jane salvaged her sense of self-worth by forming the Phillis Wheatley Foundation to provide scholarships to capable working women for job training courses in cosmetology, nursing, stenography, and domestic science, and located the headquarters across the street from the association home. As a single woman who had worked her whole life, invested conservatively, and lived frugally, Jane had amassed a small fortune; in 1960 her net worth was valued at over $400,000. Although she was declared mentally incompetent eleven years before her death in 1971, her will made careful provision for these funds. She left lump sums to five black colleges, including Ohio's Central State University, and to the Williamses' school, which had become Harbison Presbyterian School. She also established scholarships for college-bound women, with special consideration given to applicants from Ohio and South Carolina. The fund still awards scholarships in her name. The Phillis Wheatley Association is still active, providing senior housing, daycare, music lessons, and camps for youngsters, and is still located in the graceful, towering building at 4450 Cedar Avenue. In Jane's words, "Nine stories above ground, two below, it stands a monument to interracial cooperation." It also stands a monument to the woman who brought it into being.

FLORENCE ELLINWOOD ALLEN

1884–1966

A Woman of Justice

*O*hio was a battleground state for women's suffrage. In September 1912 Ohio's voters would decide on forty-one amendments to the state's revised constitution, including Amendment 23, which would strike the words "white male" from the section describing eligibility to vote and replace them with the phrase "any citizen." That summer, suffragists from the national campaign converged upon the Buckeye State to present their case to the public. Among them was a New York University law student named Florence Ellinwood Allen.

Florence was no stranger to Ohio. Her maternal grandfather, Jacob Tuckerman, was a prominent figure in northeastern Ohio, and numerous uncles and aunts and cousins lived there too. When Florence was twelve, she and her older sisters had come to study at New Lyme Academy, a college preparatory school in Ashtabula County that Tuckerman directed. She had returned in 1900, at the age of sixteen, to attend the Women's College of the Western Reserve University. Drawn by college friendships, she returned to work in Cleveland from 1906 to 1909 before moving on to law school.

Florence Ellinwood Allen

Florence was new to political organizing, however. In 1912 she had been handpicked by the beautiful and sophisticated Bostonian Maud Wood Park to serve as her assistant secretary. Florence was devoted to Park, and when a heckler interrupted at one of Park's first speeches in Columbus, Florence strode to the front of the dais to scold the offender. Park later reminded her that "one catches more flies with honey than with vinegar" and instructed her to use ladylike humor and charm to deflect the derision she was sure to encounter. After all, it was men—not women—who were to vote on the amendment.

As the summer wore on, Florence learned the art of speech-making and was dispatched to various destinations in Ohio. At circuses and county fairs, from soapbox, stage, and pulpit, twenty-seven-year-old Florence advocated women's rights, making a total of ninety-two speeches. During her travels she became acquainted with hundreds of intelligent, politically active women. She met Vadae Meekison of Henry County and Eva Epstein Shaw of Toledo, both professional lawyers. In Cleveland she met Zara DuPont and Belle Sherwin, both from families prominent in Ohio industry. In addition she met some of the leaders of the national women's movement, including Jeanette Rankin of Montana, the first woman elected to Congress.

Amendment 23 lost that September, 295,000 to 335,000, but Florence hardly felt defeated. The exhilaration of that summer remained with her through the following year at N.Y.U. After graduating and passing the New York bar exam, she considered her choices. She had spent three years studying the laws of New York, but wanted nothing more than to renew the acquaintances she had made in Ohio. She packed her belongings and moved to Cleveland. Another statewide suffrage initiative campaign was already under way there. In between speaking trips to county fairs and conventions, Florence began studying for the Ohio bar exam.

Florence Ellinwood Allen was born in Utah in 1884. Her father, Emir Allen, a classics scholar renowned for having been the first baseball player in Ohio to pitch a curve ball, had moved the family to Salt Lake City three years earlier to combat his tuberculosis. The cure worked, and Emir proved adept at everything he tried: He learned geology and surveying in order to oversee mines owned by the founder of the Cleveland *Plain Dealer* and then made them prosper even as he won the respect of the miners. Later he studied law and was eventually elected to the U. S. Congress. Florence grew up in a miner's cabin, relishing the outdoor life. She gravitated to the physically demanding chores like splitting wood and hauling water and loved to hike in the mountains. No less did she love sitting at her father's knee, learning to read ancient Greek poetry. Meanwhile, her mother, Corinne, introduced her to women's causes, which in Utah focused attention on the Mormon practice of polygamy as well as the right to vote.

Florence made friends easily and enjoyed school, where she excelled. She emerged as her peers' chosen leader and was called Cousin Jo by her classmates at the Women's College, for her resemblance to Louisa May Alcott's independent-minded character. She specialized in music and drama, assuming the male lead role in more than one play. In her "swan song" as the editor of a literary journal, she wrote an editorial condemning sororities as undemocratic—though she herself had been a member of one.

In 1904 Corinne Allen took all of her six children for a sojourn in Germany that lasted two years. Florence, who had just graduated from college, pursued her love of music with piano lessons at a conservatory and frequent trips to concerts and operas. The rest of German culture she grew to abhor, particularly its myth of the Mother as the moral force in society. She believed that the physical aspect of womanhood received far too much attention; the intellectual, far too little. By now Florence probably knew that she did not wish to marry; gradually, too, she felt unfit for her dream of becoming a concert pianist. Finally, she found an outlet for what her teachers had called her "masculine" mind, in writing music criticism for the *German Times*, a newspaper for Americans in Germany.

While the rest of the family returned to the home in Utah, Florence moved to Cleveland, renting a room just a few doors from the Tuckerman residence. She continued writing music criticism, for the Cleveland *Plain Dealer*, while teaching Greek, German, geography, American history, and music at Laurel School, a preparatory school for girls. Still, her mind hungered for meatier fare. She began taking graduate courses in political science at Western Reserve University, and when a professor suggested law school, "it came like a revelation from on high": That was what she wanted.

At that time, Western Reserve Law School did not admit women, so Florence enrolled in Chicago University Law School, the only woman in a class of one hundred. As the adage "ladies first" still applied in those days, her arrival at the door of a classroom would prompt dozens of men to stand aside while she entered, a form of attention for which she did not particularly care. She rather preferred the respect she received when the class rankings were posted, as she was invariably at or near the top. Apart from school she socialized within the circle of progressive women associated with Jane Addams' Hull House, a settlement house for newly arrived immigrants. It was through one of these connections that she was induced to move to New York and work for the League for Protection of Immigrants.

Once in New York, Florence found that Columbia University Law School would not accept women, so she enrolled at N.Y.U., which had a strong tradition of training women lawyers. She proved less than enthusiastic about social work, however. With her two younger brothers attending Yale, she felt she must pay her own way through law school, and the wages simply weren't adequate. Furthermore, the settlement house where she was expected to live was infested with bugs. She moved out, setting up house with another law school student, and found a salaried part-time position with the National College Women's Equal Suffrage League. It was this job that led her to Ohio in the summer of 1912, and prompted her return in 1913, after law school.

In 1913 Cleveland was a city full of promise for a young lawyer. The industrial boom was in full swing, and Cleveland, with its prime location on Lake Erie and the Erie Canal, was home to many major manufacturing companies, particularly in iron, steel, and petroleum. Its progressive leadership was building a municipal power plant and had created a fund for local poverty relief, the first city to do so. Unfortunately, when Florence applied for jobs at law firms, no one was hiring—women, that is. One senior partner gestured to his window, where a few snowflakes could be seen drifting down. "I wouldn't dream of sending a woman to the courthouse on a day like this," he said—to this woman whose favored recreation was mountain climbing! Eventually, Florence established her own firm and began doing volunteer work for the Cleveland Legal Aid Society. Soon, the Ohio suffragists joined her paying client list.

Florence provided the legal advice for the first suffrage victory in Ohio. After Amendment 23 failed, the strategy shifted to winning women's suffrage in likely cities. Thus, in 1916 suffragists pressured East Cleveland, a middle-class suburb, to write women's suffrage into its charter. Although the voters of East Cleveland approved the charter, the Board of Elections invalidated it. The Woman Suffrage Party immediately filed a lawsuit, which was taken up by the Ohio Supreme Court. Arguing before the court on which she herself would sit, Florence won the case. Based on this precedent, Lakewood and Columbus introduced women's suffrage in the same manner the following year.

World War I marked a turning point for Florence. To show respect for the nation's sacrifice, the suffragists temporarily silenced their demands. Eventually, the war would claim the lives of both of Florence's Yale-educated brothers. The giddy days of her youth were over. Florence's favored social cause thereafter would be world peace. Apart from that she would be pulled to the sober and demanding task of dispensing justice, a task well suited to her gifts of clear thinking and expression and her capacity for work.

In 1919 Florence—a Democrat—was appointed assistant prosecutor for Cuyahoga County under a Democratic administration. Then, in 1920, one day after Tennessee ratified the Nineteenth Amendment giving women throughout the nation the vote, Florence announced her candidacy for a judgeship on the county's Court of Common Pleas. She had only ten weeks to campaign and lacked party backing (the primary had already passed), but there were thousands of Cleveland women of both parties eager to cast their first vote for a woman. Her name became practically synonymous with the countywide registration and voter education drive, and she won the post handily. As she herself put it, she was "the beneficiary of the entire women's movement." She was also, now, its representative.

At first her eleven fellow judges on the court suggested that Florence hear all the divorce cases, a notion she firmly dismissed with the quip that, as an unmarried person, she was less qualified than most of them to rule upon such matters. Regular duty as a judge involved a rotation of criminal and civil cases, and those were the duties she was prepared to assume. In fact she went beyond the prescribed duties to do exactly what suffragists had promised women would do—clean up government in terms of both corruption and inefficiencies.

As for corruption Judge Allen turned a cold shoulder to her former colleagues in the Democratic Party who expected favors from her court. Large-boned, wearing flowing robes, Florence might have been a model for the blindfolded goddess, Justice; in her mind she owed no one anything, except for the best possible exercise of her judgment. One Democratic ward leader stated, "This Florence Allen is the worst thing that ever happened. You go into her court and ask for some usual favor and she pays no attention to it. She hardly knows who you are and if she did, it would not make any difference." In one trial, she sentenced a former judge convicted of perjury to one to ten years in the state penitentiary. Expressing her regret, she nonetheless held that "judges cannot think that they are above the law."

Government inefficiency involved more complex problem solving. For instance the Court of Common Pleas faced a long backlog of cases, and Judge Allen found that the logic determining which cases would be heard first was flawed. She tried one case in which a material witness had been held in jail three months for protective custody—a witness to the crime, not the accused! She tried another case in which accused murderers had been free on bail for months. When she attempted to address the issue of the court's docket, she encountered the next obstacle: There was no administrator or chief judge to make and communicate procedural changes. Florence spoke at mass meetings of Cleveland's women voters organized around this issue; these former suffragists in turn prevailed upon the Ohio legislature to pass a bill requiring chief judges in counties with more than one judge. Finally, she sought to try all criminal cases before summer recess, so that defendants would not spend months in jail waiting for their trials. When the other judges refused to extend the working session, Judge Allen traded her vacation time for another judge's criminal court docket and disposed of the cases herself.

Judge Allen did not remain long at the county level, however. In 1922 a late-occurring vacancy on the Ohio Supreme Court prompted another last-minute run for judgeship. The former suffragists again sprang into action. They gathered twice the number of necessary signatures on the nominating petition and formed "Florence Allen Clubs" in many counties to work for her election. The fact that Republican women readily joined these clubs so incensed the Republican Party that certain Ohio mailboxes became flooded with national party literature stressing the importance of party loyalty. Meanwhile, the state's Democrats likewise opposed Florence as a threat to their nominee. If anything, this partisan brouhaha served to endorse Judge Allen's position that the courts should be nonpartisan. The press adored her campaign for its news-worthiness, but the real force behind Florence's election was the tireless work and small cash donations of women in each of Ohio's eighty-eight counties. Defeating a popular war hero by more than 48,000 votes, Florence became the first woman in the country elected to a seat on a state supreme court.

While she sat on the Ohio Supreme Court, Judge Allen's record continued to be one of reform. She wrote opinions upholding the constitutionality of city zoning, then a progressive new concept in urban planning, and ruled on several cases involving the improvement of public schools. In a decade when labor unions were weak, Allen's opinions vindicated Ohio workers' right to a safe workplace and right to picket. And, in an era when the Ohio Supreme Court was not noted for its judicial ethics, she stood firmly for integrity, speaking out against her colleagues' infractions of the spirit of justice. For instance a case involving the construction of a sewage system in Allen County first came to the Supreme Court in 1929. The county commissioners were found to be negligent for issuing bonds for the project, then reducing the scope of the construction to a smaller area and hiring a favored company to do the work at an enhanced profit. This case returned to the Supreme Court two years later when four of Florence's colleagues were persuaded to change their minds. In her dissenting opinion, Judge Allen attacked the betrayal of public trust for the securing of private profit. Though her comments were limited to the deeds of the Allen County commissioners, their extension to her colleagues' behavior was implicit.

Florence and her network of liberal professional and political women supported Franklin Delano Roosevelt for the presidency in 1932. In 1933, as the end of Judge Allen's second term on the court approached, these women called upon prominent Ohio lawyers to write of the judge's exemplary performance and presented this testimony to President Roosevelt. The result was her 1934 appointment to the Sixth Circuit Court of Appeals, a federal court based in Cincinnati that hears appeals from cases tried in federal trial courts in Michigan, Ohio, Kentucky, and Tennessee. Florence was the first woman to serve at this level in the Federal Judiciary.

According to Florence, none of her colleagues on the federal court favored her appointment. Two swallowed their pride and wrote her congratulatory notes, but the third, Judge Hicks, remained silent. Indeed, at their first meetings, he refused to look at her. Then, one day Florence fell down a flight of stairs, landing on her chin. The judges heard of her mishap, and when she appeared in the courthouse wearing bandages and adhesive tape, Judge Moorman, who was presiding, insisted that the court postpone hearing a major case scheduled for the next day, even though lawyers and parties were already en route from Detroit. Florence replied, "Judge Moorman, I am quite aware how I look, but if I am willing to sit are you not willing to let me, rather than postpone the case?" He agreed, and the next day, Judge Hicks finally gave his female colleague a friendly glance, in appreciation of her good common sense. In the most untoward of circumstances, Florence had joined the "club."

Perhaps her most famous case was the 1938 ruling upholding the Tennessee Valley Authority, the Depression-era program that built locks and dams to control flooding and improve navigation along the Tennessee River and incidentally used the dams to supply electricity to the dwellings in the valley. Private power companies protested that the government was intervening in a sector reserved for private enterprise. Acquainted with the issues from the Cleveland experiment with municipal power, Judge Allen painstakingly sorted through the particulars and finally ruled, in an 8,000-word decision, that the TVA was within constitutional limits. This was a "watershed" victory for Roosevelt's New Deal.

As Judge Allen continued her distinguished service, many hoped that this would be a stepping-stone to the crowning achievement of a United States Supreme Court appointment. Roosevelt was mildly interested in appointing a woman Supreme Court justice, and Florence was certainly the leading candidate. But this particular "first" was not to be attained by any woman during her lifetime.

Florence, however, was hardly inclined to be disappointed. Her life had taken a most agreeable form. Her role as judge had given her an extensive on-the-job education about fields as diverse as medicine, environmental science, and industrial processes. She enjoyed several opportunities to contribute to global forums on justice, and was asked by the National Council of Churches to be a good-will lecturer in post-revolutionary Mexico. During court recess, she shared a Cleveland home with two close friends and career women, Susan Rebholz and Mary Pierce, and an assortment of cocker spaniels, which she adored. A good handful of nieces and nephews lived nearby. She owned a sixteen-acre retreat in Lake County with a shack, which in the early 1940s, she and Mary—having lost Susan to influenza in 1935—eventually refurbished into a year-round home. There, Florence returned to the outdoor activities of her youth, gathering, sawing, and splitting wood, and revived her piano skills. There also she entertained the "many fine men and women" with whom she had developed friendships over the years—friendships that she counted as the foremost reward of her work.

Toward the end of her career, Judge Allen received numerous awards and honors. In a speech at one honorary function, she argued that the primary function of the courts was not to "settle controversies," but rather something more lofty, to achieve justice, the highest of human endeavors. All her life, she had criticized deviations from this vision—for instance, law schools' emphasis on private property to the detriment of other rights. Her tenacious idealism struck a chord with those best acquainted with her work, the lawyers whose cases she had decided. At her retirement in 1959, thousands of lawyers contributed to a fund for a portrait of her to hang in the Federal Courthouse in Cincinnati; it now resides in the Statehouse in Columbus. Florence Ellinwood Allen died in 1966, survived by her companion, Mary, her loving nieces and nephews, and a large extended family of dear friends.

ELLA P. STEWART

1893–1987

Trailblazing Toledoan

$\mathcal{E}$lla had come to Toledo to visit a friend, but she was also on a scouting mission. She and her husband, William, both pharmacists, had been living in Detroit for several months, and the city did not appeal to them. It was too big—the only city where Ella had ever gotten lost. And it was getting larger and more crowded with new migrants from the South arriving each week. Toledo was similar—an industrial city—but on a smaller, more neighborly scale. One fact about the city particularly caught her attention: It had no African American drugstores. To Ella, this spelled opportunity. She had owned her own pharmacy in Pittsburgh and preferred it to working for someone else.

As she disembarked from the bus near her friend's house, Ella spotted a "For Sale" sign in the window of a stylish brick commercial building. She jotted down the pertinent information before going to meet her friend. The building in which she was interested was located on the corner of Indiana Avenue and City Park Avenue in the midst of a residential neighborhood and was adjacent to an Episcopal church. Ella contacted the real estate agent and received a tour of the first-floor store area and the spacious, high-ceilinged

Ella P. Stewart (center)

accommodations above. Then she telephoned her husband in Detroit.

"It's an ideal location for a drug store," she said. At the time, 1922, this neighborhood of Toledo known as Link's Hill was inhabited primarily by German and Irish immigrant families—working people employed in factories, but also as telephone operators, policemen, and shop girls. Surely they all needed a place to purchase medicines, candy, or a soda. "And the building is beautiful," she added.

"Buy it," was her husband's response.

And Ella did, with the money she had saved from several years of professional work as a pharmacist.

Back in Detroit, there were the usual naysayers. The pharmacy was bound to fail. Whites would not patronize a black establishment, and it was too far from the black neighborhood for most blacks to come. Ella and her husband ignored this chorus of doubters and packed up their belongings. In Toledo, they spent weeks painting and hanging wallpaper, installing a soda counter and stocking the shelves. Meanwhile, Ella met her new neighbors, and with a cheerful honesty that must have been disarming, told them that she was interested in the community and wasn't there just to make money. Finally, Stewarts Pharmacy was ready to open. Bouquets of flowers sent by friends old and new crammed the counter space. It was the moment of truth—would anybody show?

Of the crowd that thronged the store's Grand Opening, ninety percent were white. Ella had blazed her first trail in Toledo, with many more to follow. Some of the paths would lead around the world, but they would always come back to Toledo, the place Ella would henceforth call home.

Ella Nora Phillips was born on a sharecroppers' farm in northern Virginia in 1893. Her father, Henry Phillips, was the son of a Native American woman and a white man who could not marry because of Virginia's laws against interracial marriage. He married a black woman, Ella's mother, Eliza Carr. Ella and her sisters and brothers grew up playing with children of all races, but were forced to attend a segregated elementary school. Her father did all he could to counter the negative messages his children received from this treatment.

One day as they were racing turtles they'd found in a stream, Henry Phillips took the opportunity to teach his children a lesson. "Look at those turtles," he said. "As long as they're willing to sit, they can stay safe and all tucked in, but as soon as they want to get anyplace they've got to stick their necks out. That's the way it is going to be with you. If you want to get someplace you're going to have to stick your necks out." This lesson stayed with Ella all her life.

Ella was a gifted student, first in her grade school classes. When she was twelve, she was sent to a school in West Virginia, the nearest secondary school that would accept black students. Four years later, she received a scholarship to attend Simmons College in Boston for teacher training. However, she changed her plans for a classmate, Charles Myers, who had moved to Pittsburgh to become a chauffeur. She married Charles in Pittsburgh and gave birth to a daughter, Virginia, who died of whooping cough two-and-a-half years later, in 1912. Approaching age twenty, Ella had the burden—or the opportunity—of starting over. Her friends urged her to put her talents to use, so Ella found a job as a bookkeeper for a nearby drug store. Observing the work of the pharmacists and deciding that she herself could do it, she "stuck her neck out" and enrolled in the University of Pittsburgh's College of Pharmacy. Although she encountered prejudice as the first black student in the program, she also earned respect and graduated with high marks and good recommendations, becoming one of the first black women pharmacists in the nation.

Within a short time, Ella was managing a drug store in Braddock, then a small town a few miles east of Pittsburgh. She combined this daytime work with night work as the pharmacist of Braddock General Hospital. After four years of this grueling schedule, she had managed to purchase the drug store business but had lost her marriage. She and Charles were divorced. In 1920 she decided to take an extended trip home to Virginia and hired an interim manager, William Stewart, a black man who had graduated from the College of Pharmacy the same year she had enrolled. Shortly after she returned to Pittsburgh, they were married with the understanding that they would practice as equal partners. Ella sold the pharmacy, and they moved to Youngstown, Ohio.

It is unclear exactly what brought the couple from Pittsburgh to Youngstown in 1920, and what took them to Detroit in 1922. One story is often repeated about their stay in Youngstown, however. Ella announced to her friends that she was applying to Youngstown City Hospital, which had advertised for a pharmacist.

"Don't bother," the doubters told her. "They won't even hire a Negro to sweep the floor."

But Ella had confidence in herself and a knack for approaching such situations. She landed the job and thereby lit a trail. When she left two years later, there were forty African Americans working at Youngstown City Hospital!

Ella kept her promise to the neighborhood in Toledo. She became the eyes and ears—and the legs—of the community, looking out for anyone who might need help, then doing what needed to be done. The most obviously needy were the African American migrants arriving from the rural South. Ella formed the Enterprise Charity Club, whose mission was to help these migrants understand urban ways. Most had lived in log cabins on a farm; she taught them to sew curtains and mow their lawns. In addition, she approached local businesses and persuaded them to sell damaged or overstock furniture and household goods at wholesale prices, to help furnish the newcomers' homes. Such actions quickly made her a leader: "I got to be popular with the women because I knew so many people, because I had nerve enough to go and make an appointment to see the manager of the various stores."

Her reception on these visits did not always begin warmly. She made appointments by telephone; her arrival in the flesh often engendered surprise and resistance. "Are you sure you have an appointment?" the receptionist would ask.

"Oh, yes, I have an appointment," Ella would answer, halfway amused at the scene her dark-skinned presence was creating.

She might have to wait for long stretches of time until it became clear that she fully intended to keep her appointment. When she was finally received, her demeanor was just as pleasant as it had been to begin with. This was how Ella operated and how she moved the city forward.

Ella's husband, who became widely known as Doc Stewart, liked to tease her that she was doing more social work than pharmacy work, for which she had been trained. And he was right. In fact the two were a perfect team. In his role as pharmacist, Doc became the confidant of many of his customers. He would learn the latest family news and gossip for Ella to use in her social work. Doc might discover, for example, that a husband was beating his wife, and Ella would confer with the women of her club to see what could be done.

Ella became very involved with the community children. She volunteered to lead an African American group of Girl Reserves, a YWCA program similar to Girl Scouts. Most of the troops met at the YWCA, but the facility did not at that time allow blacks inside. Ella made an appointment with the proper authorities to discuss her dilemma and soon had permission for her group to meet there.

Ella opened yet another door in the League of Women Voters, the organization formed by former suffragists after women won the vote. As soon as Ella heard of a Toledo chapter forming, she applied for admission, the only black Toledoan to do so. Her application stirred strong debate, until a Jewish woman named Levinson took up her cause. At the first few meetings, Ella noted that some of the women refused to smile at her, but she chose not to care; she knew she belonged, as an active, involved woman of Toledo, and as a human being. As always, her intelligent good humor and tolerance eventually prevailed over the initial prejudice.

Ella took a special, almost mischievous delight in being the exception to the rule; her goal, however, was to challenge and to change the rules. Thus, when the movie ushers allowed her to sit on the first floor but forced other blacks into the balcony, she instructed all her employees to tell the ushers they were her nephews and nieces. Their friends joined in this ruse, and soon enough, the movie theater was effectively integrated.

Indeed, as the years passed and the neighborhood matured, Ella became a surrogate mother or aunt to many of the neighborhood children. She joined the League of City Mothers because, explained Ella, she felt she "really had a great many children." She used her contacts to arrange job interviews for her "children" and make sure they were given due courtesies as employees. If a child landed in jail, she would visit him there. If a student received poor grades at Toledo University, she would visit with the instructor to determine whether racial prejudice was the cause, and if it was, she would gently persuade the instructor to see his error. Finally, whenever she or other black Toledoans found a pattern of discrimination, she would quietly report them to her friend, Grove Patterson, editor-in-chief of the Toledo *Blade*, and he would discuss the problem in the public forum of his newspaper's editorial pages.

For this work she was asked to be a founding member of Toledo's Board of Community Relations.

As effective as Ella was on behalf of her black customers, she and Doc retained their German customers from the early days. Long after they had left the neighborhood, these white immigrants would come across town into what had become a black neighborhood, just to spend their money at Stewarts Pharmacy and visit with Doc. Hospitality was clearly part of the Stewarts' appeal. Above the pharmacy were nine rooms, including spare bedrooms that, from the mid 1920s to 1945, were occupied at one time or another by the shining lights of their race. Paul Robeson and Marian Anderson, world-renowned singers, Mary McLeod Bethune, member of the Roosevelts' unofficial "black cabinet," W. E. B. Dubois, founder of the NAACP, and Carter Woodson, historian and founder of Black History Month, all stayed at the Stewarts' home. And in 1932 Ella was influential in introducing the twenty-three-year-old blind jazz artist and Toledo native, Art Tatum, to the nationally known vocalist, Adelaide Hall, who needed a pianist for her upcoming New York tour; Tatum went on to become a jazz legend.

Ella's extensive club activity and her budding friendship with Mary McLeod Bethune led naturally to participation in the National Association of Colored Women (NACW), which supported the work of African American club women in improving conditions for blacks at the local level. As a friend of Bethune, she met Eleanor Roosevelt and participated in some of the discussions held by the president's cabinet of advisers on racial issues. In 1945 she and Doc sold the pharmacy so that she could devote more time to club work, and in 1948 she was elected president of the NACW, serving two two-year terms and making weekly trips to the nation's capital in this capacity. Each year, she made a special point of visiting the United Nations building in New York. Listening from the viewing gallery, she became fascinated by the concept of human rights. In her mind, the struggles of African Americans in Toledo and elsewhere were suddenly and profoundly linked to struggles of people all over the world. She began to think and talk in terms of the "human family": "I belong to the human family, and I believe that all their goals are my goals."

In 1951 Ella was chosen to be a delegate to the International Conference of Women of the World, held in Greece. She cherished this opportunity to meet distant members of her "human family," and immediately invited all these new friends to visit her in Toledo. The gesture extended especially to her hosts: At her invitation the King and Queen of Greece came to Toledo in 1953. About the same time, she became involved in the Pan Pacific South East Asia Women's Association (PPSEAWA), a U.N. organization devoted to "strengthening the bonds of peace by founding a friendship and better understanding among women." This involvement resulted in trips to Philippines, Japan, Australia, Tonga, Hawaii, Korea, and Samoa, and reciprocal visits by guests from those countries. The Toledo chapter of PPSEAWA International is still a thriving entity. Between 1953 and 1956 she was invited by the U.S. State Department on several goodwill tours to the principal cities of Pakistan, India, Ceylon, Indonesia, and the Philippines to explain America and discuss women's roles and education.

This international work kept Ella young. In 1963, at the age of seventy, she was appointed as a commissioner for the United Nations Education Scientific and Cultural Organization (UNESCO). In 1964 she stated her philosophy for this work: "Women of the world must be down in the front lines to defend humanity. This is our task if we are to preserve our heritage for future generations." UNESCO took her to new places in the Western Hemisphere, such as Haiti, Jamaica, Cuba, and Mexico. She was particularly affected by the sights of suffering humanity in Haiti, and was deeply honored when the Haitian ambassador came to visit her in Toledo.

In all her international work, Ella was not just trail blazing; she was putting Toledo on the map. Her proudest moment, in 1961, was wholly local: Toledo's school board members made the rare decision to honor a living person and voted to name a new elementary school the Ella P. Stewart School. Ella swore that she wished they hadn't, but after the ground breaking, she visited the construction site every day to observe the building's progress. Located at Avondale Avenue and Elizabeth Street, a short distance from the old pharmacy, its completion marked a proud moment for Toledo's African Americans. As one speaker said, "We have honored ourselves by honoring her." Being the school "mother" allowed Ella to add more children to her ever-expanding "family." She visited frequently, offered scholarships, helped put together African American cultural programs, and on one occasion, purchased tickets for the entire sixth grade to see the Harlem Boys Choir. One of the pupils described her influence this way: "She says smile and lift your head up and think good of yourself."

Despite her outstanding achievements Ella faced petty discrimination even in the final decades of her life. In 1957 her invitation to a ceremony honoring Virginia's distinguished sons and daughters was revoked when it was discovered that she was African American. Her Toledo friends responded to this insult by planning a large testimonial dinner, attended by both blacks and whites. When, at the age of eighty-seven, she entered a nursing home in 1980, she was surprised to find the same unenlightened attitudes among the staff and residents.

Ella was a rare woman who combined an insatiable curiosity with a keen desire to serve. She identified deeply with African Americans and their struggles, but also with all people everywhere.

She accomplished so much because she always saw her glass as half full rather than half empty. The smiles she wears in photographs seem to originate deep within her. Ella's enthusiastic hospitality, tireless work, and irrepressible love for her "human family" made a lasting impression on Ohio's urban landscape. She passed away in 1987, but is still remembered by her young friends in Toledo.

LOIS LENSKI
1893–1974

Collaborator with Children

*Y*oung Lois loved Christmas, as most children do. Each Christmas Eve, the Lutheran church in the very small town of Anna, Ohio, where her father was the pastor, held a special service. As the children entered the sanctuary, they would see the huge Christmas tree illuminated by candles. Beside the tree were two men, standing like sentries. They each held a bucket of water and a long pole with a sponge attached to extinguish any candles that might begin to spit and sputter dangerously. Beneath the tree were presents—presents for every child in the parish.

After all of the children had recited their memorized pieces, it was time to distribute the gifts. When her age group's turn came, Lois approached the tree and was handed an orange. In the cold and snow of December, it felt like a miracle from another world, round as a ball in her hands. Then, she received a box of candy. She remembered this delicious candy from last year! Finally, a book was placed in her hands—a gift that would last. She looked at the title with ebbing hope. Barely visible in the dim light, she read *From Poverty to Riches,* and her heart sank. Back at her family's pew, she consulted her siblings. They too had received duds, narratives sure

Lois Lenski

to be all about "goodness" by authors who seemed to have forgotten what childhood was all about. "Who picks these, anyway?" Lois wondered and then returned to watching the men with the sponges.

At home there were more preparations. When bedtime came, Lois and her younger sister Miriam decided to wear their clothes to bed, so they could be ready when the call came in the morning. As their parents rummaged in the closet for the gifts they'd hidden, the children savored their anticipation, talking and giggling until their father came in to silence them. Afterward, more giggling and whispering. Finally, they fell asleep, only to be wakened at 3:00 A.M. by their brothers' words: "Get up! It's Christmas!" In spite of their parents' best efforts to quiet them, the entire family was up within the hour.

The Reverend Lenski's lighting of the big coal lamp was the children's signal to dash downstairs and begin tearing through the packages. Each had a chair where his or her gifts were piled. Saving the square, flat packages for last, Lois found first a pair of mittens, then some doll clothing. Finally, she tore open the wrapping to this year's book.

"*Little Women!*" she exclaimed.

"*Arabian Nights!*" said her older sister, Esther, holding up a thick volume.

"*Swiss Family Robinson!* Edgar Allan Poe!" her brothers chimed in.

"*The ... Five ... Little ... Peppers... and How they Grew!*" said little Miriam.

Now these were real books—books with characters who seemed to live and breathe, books that could take you somewhere. Through all the special things that came next—iced cinnamon rolls, tolling bells, and Christmas carols in church—the true promise of Christmas for Lois lay on the horizon. That promise was the long afternoon, when she could sprawl about the house poring through her new literary treasure. The books were swapped and shared through the years, and with subscriptions to *Harper's*, *Century*, *Scribner's*, *Atlantic Monthly*, *Women's Home Companion* and *Youths' Companion*, there was always plenty of quality literature in the Lenski house.

Decades later, Lois Lenski's books—dozens of them, all high-quality, well-researched, and inspired by real children—would provide the same anticipation and joy to new generations of boys and girls.

Except for the croup at age three and pneumonia at age eight, Lois had a blessed childhood. Born in Springfield, Ohio, in 1893, she was the fourth of five children of Marietta Young, a native of the Columbus area, and Richard Lenski, a native of what was then called Prussia, in Eastern Europe. The parents met when Lenski attended the Lutheran Seminary at Capital University in Columbus. His first parish was in Springfield, and this is where Lois was born. When she was six, the family moved to Anna, Ohio, population 200, in Shelby County. In her autobiography, Lois describes Anna as "the perfect child's town": "It had no particular beauty or grace, but it soon became my own, a compound of sights and sounds and smells and buildings and people that became a part of me." She knew every person, every street and alley, every tree and flowerbed.

The turn of the century was a time of hard, simple work in small-town Ohio. People still traveled by horse and buggy and lived self-sufficiently for the most part, even in town. Lois's mother kept a garden and canned produce for the winter. She hauled water year-round from an outdoor pump, boiled the family's clothes in a big pot on their wood-fueled kitchen stove, and sewed the children's outfits, along with preparing meals and shopping. Her father's meager salary was supplemented by gifts of livestock and assorted items that the parishioners would round up every so often and deliver to their house in a surprise visit.

The family's pleasures were simple, as well, but no less abundant: popping popcorn, shelling nuts, pulling taffy, singing, sledding, playing in the barn, scribbling on scraps of paper retrieved from their father's wastepaper basket, and, of course, reading. Work and play merged in seasonal rituals such as autumn threshing, when the whole community—men, women, and children—gathered at one farm to prepare their wheat crop for market, separating the grain from the straw.

Not all of Lois's childhood experiences were pleasant ones. As a pastor's child, she often went with her family to the homes of strangers. Once, playing hide-and-seek with her siblings on such a visit, she came upon an old log cabin. Curious, she peered through the iron bars covering its windows—right into the bloodshot eyes of a wild-haired woman, whom she believed to be a witch. In fact the woman was mentally ill; in that era, such "treatment" of family members was acceptable. On another occasion, she listened to her father console the daughter of a man who had hanged himself earlier that day.

Lois found herself, as many future authors do, to be very much the observer growing up. She studied people to figure out what they thought and what motivated their actions. Her mind and heart were inclusive: She used these observations not to judge but to understand others better. When her sisters improvised plays for their dolls or acted out dramas themselves, Lois was the audience or exercised her creative impulse in designing and stitching clothes for the dolls. She sent her best work to "Aunt Janet," the editor of the children's page of the *Woman's Home Companion,* and imagined becoming a dressmaker. Apart from these activities, she was arts-deprived. The art classes at the public schools she attended taught her little more than how to copy professional artists' drawings.

After Lois's 1911 graduation from the high school in Sidney, Ohio, a stroke of luck enabled her to continue her education: Her father accepted a teaching post at Capital University, and the family moved to Bexley, a suburb of Columbus. Had she not lived with her parents, Lois could not have afforded college, and there were no colleges in Shelby County. Capital did not then admit women, so she attended Ohio State University across town—which offered her a wider range of experiences. In addition to education classes—like most coeds of the time, Lois planned to teach—she took art, engineering, French, and German. On Saturdays she invited neighbor children over for storytelling. To find more stories to tell, she translated French and German folktales into English. In the summers she worked for the city Department of Recreation as a crafts counselor at one of their playgrounds.

It seems natural that Lois would have applied for a teaching position when she graduated. She loved children, she was well qualified, and she needed the income. Conversely, it might seem out-of-character for this cautious A-student to have tossed that plan aside for art school in New York City—but that is exactly what Lois did. The taste of real arts education she received at Ohio State University had shown her how much more there was to discover. Moreover, one of her instructors had told her of the Art Students League, an informal program with a $5 monthly tuition from which the Columbus painter Alice Schille had recently graduated.

Lois came to New York in 1915 with $300 in the bank. Rooming with other cash-strapped art students, she attended classes for half the day and spent the other half employed painting lampshades, composing rhymes for greeting cards, and drawing fashion illustrations for advertisements. That first summer she returned to her family's home in Bexley to sell flowers from their garden to downtown shops. She turned down a teaching offer from a Lutheran school in order to return for a second year of art school, adding to her schedule a free night course in illustration at the nearby School of Industrial Arts. This course, taught by Arthur Covey, a large, angular, "stuttery" man, would change the course of her life, in more ways than one. In March 1917 Lois observed in her diary that Covey had been "taking a little notice of [her] lately, to *his* surprise." In May, when Covey's wife died after the birth of a baby boy, she wrote, "What will he do with those two young-sters—big, awkward, helpless man that he is!" Later that year, he invited Lois to become his assistant, painting murals for depart-ment store window displays.

This professional relationship lasted for three years. Lois turned down yet another offer to teach—this time at a prestigious New York private school, attended by "Rockefellers and Gould youngsters," and in 1920 traveled to London to continue her stud-ies. Here, she won a publisher's contract to illustrate a children's book. Offered the opportunity to accompany an older woman on a trip to Italy, she eagerly accepted it, filling several sketchbooks with scenes of ancient hillside villages. Then, as she wrote at that time, she returned to New York and took the "fatal step," marry-ing Arthur Covey. Rather than abandon her career, she wrote the she "hope[d] to prove that a woman (or at least this one woman) can do two jobs at once!" She felt that, as a single father, Covey had an "impossible load" and wished to take that load upon herself.

Lois got her wish. During the first years of her marriage she felt continually rundown from her household labors, which included entertaining, as well as housework, gardening, and child care. The consolation was her developing relationship with the children: Margaret, age twelve, who became like a younger sister to her, and Laird, the four-year-old boy who had lost his mother at birth—a terrified, tantrum-prone child whom Lois rehabilitated with her patient understanding.

Lois's new roles gave her little time to paint. Covey's response to her dilemma between home and career was simply to tell her, "Your job is the home and the children." Undaunted, Lois took to sketching in her spare moments, filling one after the next notebook with pencil drawings. She took sketching trips to the beach and visited an art-school friend in North Carolina, sketching all she saw. She drew the illustrations for several children's books. When publishers told her that her style did not match their books, she decided to write her own. In 1926 she wrote and illustrated *Skipping Village*, her first children's book, based on memories from her childhood. *A Little Girl of 1900* followed. In Lois's words:

> Suddenly the making of books became terribly important, more important than painting pictures. Books were living things, they went into the hands of children, and if they were worthwhile, they would be loved and enjoyed—and they could shape lives.

The birth of her own son, Stephen, in 1929 gave Lois the final push in this direction. She would see every single phase of this child's development and begin to see the world from a child's perspective. Her first book for Stephen, at age two, was a picture book, *The Little Family*. At four years, his favorite game was to pretend that his wagon or tricycle was a real car; in response she wrote *The Little Car*. The Stephen character in that book, "Mr. Small," guided Lois's next few books, including *The Little Train* and *The Little Airplane*. These books did not personify the inanimate object in a childish way; instead, they were about the grownup roles—car driver, engineer, pilot—that fascinated Stephen and his friends. Lois's goal, first and last, was to write books that *appealed* to children; thus, her son became her most trusted consultant, editor, and critic.

In 1929, the year of Stephen's birth, the Coveys had moved to an old Connecticut farmhouse that lacked plumbing and reliable electrical power. If this rustic quaintness meant more work for Lois, she did not let it slow her progress. She claimed an old shop building high on a hill for her studio and mused upon the changes modernization was bringing as she watched the adjacent hayfields being mowed on the one side by oxen or horses, on the other by a tractor. Such musings inspired her next series of books, which took historical life as their subject.

Lois excelled at this. She conducted months of scholarly research before launching into a work of historical fiction, reading old diaries, letters, newspapers, and magazines of the period to understand the culture she was to represent in each particular work. For instance, Lois found the title of her book about a Connecticut family's trek to Ohio in 1811, *A Going to the Westward*, in a letter a Connecticut boy wrote to his cousin in New Connecticut, Ohio. Part of her research throughout the series focused on the history of childhood itself, for what is expected of children has changed so very much during America's history. The most acclaimed volume in this series was *Indian Captive: The Story of Mary Jemison*. This narrative of a girl captured and raised by Seneca Indians was ahead of its time in terms of its depth, accuracy and respectful tone toward the native culture.

Life in the drafty old house finally caught up with Lois's health in the 1940s, when her doctor recommended that she spend winters in the South. Her first real journey south—to Florida— was an awakening: The lives of children in Florida were far different from any Ohio or Connecticut childhood. She began talking with these children about their experiences. The result was a book, *Strawberry Girl*, about a girl who was growing strawberries in a region of Florida formerly given over to open-range ranching. The central conflict was with a malicious, drunken neighbor, who insisted on running his cattle and hogs over her fields, and his sons, who caused trouble in school. Lois defended the inclusion of such characters in her books: "To leave them out and to pretend that such things never happen would be to present a false picture." Again, she remembered the lesson of her Christmas past. This story won Lois the Newbery Medal for excellence in children's literature.

With *Strawberry Girl* Lois began a new series of books based on regional differences. Lois wanted to teach children to understand and accept people who were different from them. In particular she wanted to instill respect for simple ways of life, "to point out that people of character, people who are guided by spiritual values, come often from simple surroundings, and are worthy of our admiration and even our emulation." Like the regionalists of the time—Thomas Hart Benton, Doris Lee, Grant Wood, whose work her own drawings resembled—she felt that excitement need not be "manufactured," "new," or imported from Europe, but that it is inherent in the various American traditions, rooted in the American soil. Furthermore, she feared that the changes in American society were depriving children of vital experiences with the life-giving natural world. And, as their parents traded small-town, farm life for jobs in the city, children became sheltered from adult spheres of work and thereby were deprived of the growth of mind that such contact brings. Lois hoped that her regional books could do something to counter this trend.

Most of all, Lois, like a child, was curious about the different regions of America. Upon arriving in a place, she would set out on foot carrying a campstool and her bag of materials until she found a picturesque scene to sketch. Invariably, children would approach her to see what she was doing. She would pepper them with questions, "What do your fathers do? What is that machine for?" Soon enough, she would have a delighted embassy of children, leading her from one home to the next, informing her of everything she needed to know to re-create a world, whether bayou or prairie or peanut farm. Lois would fill whole notebooks with notes and sketches. She recorded speech patterns, expressions, places and faces, different ways of life. Children responded to the depictions of real life in her books, especially her clear-eyed view of poverty, and they began to think their humble lives might be of interest, too. Lois received invitations from students in other regions to come visit *their* homes and write about *their* lives, and almost always accepted them.

Traveling and writing was Lois's life, and she lived most of it alone. She and her husband—now a well-known mural painter—had long since ceased sharing their work. Still, they continued to live together in Connecticut and enjoy the visits of grandchildren. Lois's last extended "collaboration" was with a boy named Davy, who came to her three summers in a row, beginning in 1943, as a foster child badly in need of love. For weeks on end, he would cry, despite Lois's best efforts to entertain and comfort him. Then, one day, he simply dried his tears and began to follow her around the house and yard, cheerily calling her "Lo-Lo." Lois's joy at this change in his outlook was expressed in a series of Davy books, picture books made for—and with—him.

Lois received numerous awards in her life, in addition to the coveted Newbery Medal. Her advice to aspiring writers was always, "Get out of yourself . . . Get out of your ivory tower, get out of the safe, protected campus world . . . and become interested in other people and their concerns."

In the late 1950s the Coveys finally moved permanently to Florida, but neither artist retired. Arthur Covey died in 1960. Lois continued researching, writing, and making young friends until the age of eighty. During her incredibly productive life, she published almost one hundred books, and illustrated fifty more. Her contribution to children's literature is indisputable. Her work translates scholarly historical and sociological research into insights for children. In addition, she was one of the first American educators to recognize the importance of multicultural children's literature.

And, of course, Lois had proved that "this one woman" could indeed do two jobs at once! Her family and her readership both benefited from the division—and the fruitful, hopeful harmony—of her labors. In the end, Lois's most important collaboration was with the wide-eyed, curious little girl of Anna, Ohio.

DOROTHY FULDHEIM

1893–1989

Cleveland's Media Doyenne

*I*t was 1934, and Dorothy Fuldheim was in Europe to gain a firsthand understanding of the deepening crisis there brought on by the global Depression. Her audiences on the national lecture circuit, she felt, deserved more than just recycled information. She was interested particularly in Germany, which in 1933 had elected a new chancellor. Germany also held special personal interest to Dorothy because her parents had emigrated from Germany in the 1880s.

On a late-night stroll after her arrival in Hamburg, Dorothy noticed a large number of prostitutes on the streets and was surprised when one of them approached her. The woman explained in German that she was hungry. "Could you buy me a sandwich?" she asked.

Dorothy took pity on the woman and brought her to the hotel restaurant where she learned of the woman's dreadful situation— her disabled mother, her brutal father, and her hard luck in her shameful profession. Then, suddenly, the woman's mood changed.

"I'm going to get out of this life," she said.

THE CLEVELAND PRESS COLLECTION, CLEVELAND STATE UNIVERSITY LIBRARY

Dorothy Fuldheim

When Dorothy asked how, the woman spoke of Hitler: "He's going to get jobs for all of us."

Dorothy wondered to herself what made this Hitler so convincing.

Several days later, she was on a street in Dresden when another woman approached her—this one a part-time English tutor—commenting on her American-made shoes. As they talked, this educated woman repeated the Nazis' promise of jobs. "Have you never heard Adolph Hitler speak?" the woman asked with disbelief, then invited Dorothy to a speech Hitler was to make that night. In return for the favor, Dorothy bought her dinner and gave her the shoes (which pinched her feet). At the evening's event Dorothy was astonished at what seemed to her a blustering, ridiculous-looking man. But she was disturbed at the roar of approval that rose from the crowd, especially whenever Hitler mentioned the Jews.

Dorothy decided to follow Hitler to Munich for a chance to interview him. She was in his office negotiating an appointment with his secretary when he entered. Seizing the opportunity, Dorothy approached him directly, praising his Dresden perform-ance in halting German. He granted her an on-the-spot interview. When she asked how he saw Germany's role, he said, "To be the great power of Europe."

"But Germany tried that in the war and was defeated," reminded Dorothy.

He glared at her. "*Der Juden!* They were responsible for our defeat."

"Herr Hitler," Dorothy said, rather saucily, "shall I tell the Americans that the Jews were responsible for Germany's defeat, and the Allies had no part in it?"

Hitler mentioned "international Jewish bankers," then domi-nated the rest of the interview with a rehash of his previous night's rant. Having heard enough, Dorothy simply watched him. He was carrying a riding whip that he would periodically slap against his boots. She fancied him a sinister "circus master."

"Luckily, he didn't know I was Jewish," she commented later.

Dorothy returned to Germany five times in the 1930s to monitor and report on the political situation. In 1937, less than a year before Hitler annexed Austria and set up the first concen-tration camp, she tried to warn the American public of the dan-gers this megalomaniac posed. Unfortunately, her speeches on the subject were considered overdramatic. Her voice was simply not heeded.

Ten years later, with the founding of Cleveland's first TV station, fifty-four-year-old Dorothy Fuldheim would be on her way to becoming one of the most trusted voices in Cleveland. For thirty-seven years she appeared daily on WEWS, first as the anchorwoman of the news show, then as a talk show host and an editorialist. Disagree with her, viewers might—but they still tuned in, and Dorothy became a national celebrity. After all, there were few public figures with Dorothy's breadth of experience, her blunt honesty, and her incorruptible values.

Dorothy Violet Schnell was born to Herman and Bertha Schnell in Passaic, New Jersey. When she was seven, the family moved to Milwaukee, hoping to escape poverty. Dorothy walked to school with holes in her shoes and remembered wearing dresses made by her mother out of old curtains. Her childhood was dominated by cold and hunger—and by books. In return for performing a variety of errands, Dorothy had free access to the shelf of romance novels kept on the third-floor porch of her next-door neighbor, who, incidentally, ran a brothel from her apartment. Her mother did not fear her corruption: To the Schnells reading was a highly valued activity, regardless of the circumstances. Eventually, Dorothy discovered the public library and became a twice-a-week patron. Her large vocabulary prompted the taunt of "dictionary swallower" from her schoolmates, but this did not deter her.

Herman Schnell also played a role in her intellectual development. To stimulate his mind after working long hours at menial jobs, he would attend the local court and observe the judicial proceedings. Dorothy often accompanied him on these jaunts, honing her own mind while unconsciously absorbing the basics of dramatic oratory.

After graduating from high school and the Milwaukee Normal College, Dorothy taught elementary school for one year, but "felt confined" by this life. She later explained, "I had all this emotion within me and had to find a release for it." With a dramatic flair epitomized by her flaming red hair, she took up acting, performing on the Milwaukee-Chicago arena theater circuit from 1917 to 1918.

In one such production, Dorothy played the mother of a boy who dies in battle. Evidently, she delivered her lines about the sense-lessness of war with such fervor that the great Chicago reformer Jane Addams was convinced from her seat in the audience that the cause was Dorothy's own—or could be. Addams, who had founded the first settlement house in Chicago, was at the time devoting most of her efforts to the peace movement and needed a captivating speaker to liven up an upcoming Philadelphia fund-raiser. "You have a week to prepare," she told a flabbergasted and somewhat awestruck Dorothy. One week later, Dorothy delivered an acclaimed speech interlaced with poetry and dramatic enactment.

That same year, 1918, Dorothy married Milton Fuldheim, a graduate of a Cleveland law school, and moved to Ohio. Their first and only child, Dorothy Louise, followed soon thereafter. One day, Dorothy was taking a stroll through their new neighborhood of Cleveland Heights, when she was stopped by a woman who seemed to recognize her. Indeed, the woman had seen her speak in Philadelphia and had been very impressed. Could Dorothy give a book review for the City Women's Club of Cleveland? Something dramatic, entertaining—for a fee, of course.

Dorothy's book review was a success, and many more such engagements followed. Soon enough, she was reading and drama-tizing twelve books a week to multiple audiences, some as large as 1,800, both in and around Cleveland. She never brought notes to her performances, or for that matter, planned in any detail what she would say. Rather, with her tenacious memory and her ability to bring characters to life, she would simply assume the novel's differ-ent character roles and enact key moments of the book. She began lecturing on other topics of currency, and by the late 1920s was a prominent lecturer on the national lyceum circuit. Every lecture—no matter how factually based—became a performance shaped by Dorothy's dramatic instincts.

Dorothy's numerous trips to Europe in the 1930s gave her fresh material for her talks. At the same time, she entered the new field of radio. In the late 1930s Dorothy recorded more than one hundred hour-long radio shows in which she dramatized the life story of a famous person, be it Marie Antoinette, Cleopatra, or Lenin. Again she worked extemporaneously, without notes even, her spontaneous use of detail captivating her greatly expanded audience. Her varied experiences also lent her an aura of *gravitas* as she entered the field of radio news. WJW radio hired her for news commentary at the height of World War II in 1943—the most serious of times for our country and the world. ABC News noticed her talent and hired her for brief editorial and news commentary following their national Saturday afternoon broadcasts of the opera. Dorothy would take an overnight train to New York to record these weekly spots.

The post-war era saw the rise of a new communications technology, television. In 1947 Cleveland, then the sixth-largest city in the United States, became home to the eleventh television station in the country, WEWS-TV5, owned by the Scripps-Howard newspaper company. Dorothy's popularity in the Cleveland area and her reputation as one of the nation's top lecturers made her— at age fifty-four—the station manager's first choice for a news anchor, although that term had not yet been coined. At first the sponsors expected her to read from a script that someone else had written. "When I told them that wasn't what I did, they said, 'Hell, let her do what she wants. We're not going to keep her anyhow.'" They thought Dorothy, with her "dictionary-swallowing" vocabulary, was too sophisticated for the meat-and-potatoes Cleveland audience. Of course they were wrong.

The sponsors forgot that Dorothy had spent the first two decades of her life in tattered and threadbare clothes. "Everyone ought to have been born poor," she liked to say. "You have more respect for people when you become successful." She connected with people and people's stories and delivered the news as stories, each with its own emotional dimension. A tragic accident should arouse the viewers' sorrow; a political scandal, their ire. She trusted that her dramatic presentation of the news would make important information and debate accessible to all citizens of Cleveland.

Dorothy anchored the fifteen-minute WEWS newscast for fourteen years. She also conducted interviews with national celebrities who had engagements in Cleveland. She interviewed Edward, the Duke of Windsor, who had given up the English throne to marry the woman he loved, a twice-divorced American. Dorothy considered him the most romantic figure of the age. She requested and received an interview with Joseph McCarthy, the Wisconsin senator whose Communist witch-hunts ruined many careers. Over her guest's seat, Dorothy had posted the quote, "I may disapprove of what you say, but I will defend to the death your right to say it." Though she disagreed with McCarthy, she conceded that he possessed personal charm.

When the station expanded in 1957, Dorothy's talents were employed in the pioneering variety talk-show format of *The One O'Clock Club*. The show, hosted by Dorothy and Bill Gordon, was aired live before a live studio audience with a live studio orchestra. In this setting, Dorothy could fully cultivate her sense of glamour and theatricality; her flamboyant entrance, sashaying on the set in an elaborate gown, became an event in itself. As a personality she was a hit: She convulsed audiences with her staged ignorance about sports, such as confusing touchdowns with home runs, and she professed to know nothing about cooking or cleaning house, either. Her comedic side had the appeal of her redheaded contemporary, Lucille Ball, and seemed to soften the blow of the formidable intellect she displayed with her spellbinding book reviews and interviews. *The One O'Clock Club* made Dorothy a Cleveland legend, and in 1964 when national competitors including Merv Griffin's show took its place, WEWS simply could not retire her. At the age of seventy-one, Dorothy began doing two-a-day editorial features.

An actress at heart, Dorothy lived by the maxim that "the show must go on." Once, she tripped on a TV camera cable offstage, falling and breaking her arm. The physical pain did not prevent her from taking her place on the set minutes later. She was also offstage when she heard the news of President John F. Kennedy's assassination. After clutching her colleagues for support, she went on to host the *One O'Clock Show*—all one-and-a-half hours of it. Not that Dorothy could not be spontaneous. In a live interview with Jerry Rubin, the 1960s rabble-rouser, she took offense at his reference to "pigs" (policemen) and ordered him out of the studio.

On one occasion, however, she shared the full gamut of her emotions with Cleveland's viewing audience. The day was May 4, 1970. From inside her WEWS office, Dorothy heard the words "Kent State" and rushed to the scene in a WEWS vehicle. When she arrived, thirteen students lay on the ground, shot by National Guardsmen who had been called in to protect campus property against the students Governor James Rhodes called "outside agitators" and who had set fire to the university's R.O.T.C. headquarters two days before. In fact all of those shot on May 4 were Kent State students, many of them innocent bystanders. Four of them died on the spot from gunshot wounds. Dorothy's instincts revolted in horror. The students were unarmed. They could have been controlled without gunfire. She returned to the TV studio and prepared her statement. On the air, she described the scene she had encountered and, through tears of sorrow and rage, denounced the Guard's actions as murder.

That night WEWS received hundreds of phone calls. The vast majority decried Dorothy's instincts. "They should have killed more of 'em" was the regrettable response from some. Those were difficult times in America. The expansion of U. S. bombing into Cambodia had led to increasingly militant protests, and the nation's collective nerves were fraught with tension. Her own spirit crumpled and her reputation trashed, Dorothy offered her resignation, but her boss would not have it. "You are nine feet tall," he assured her. In fact the crisis did pass—to be replaced, of course, by others. Dorothy remained in her popular editorial slots, offering trenchant comments on Watergate, skyrocketing gas prices, and other events of the 1970s.

Crisis had come and gone in Dorothy's personal life, as well, but some events would take a permanent toll. Her husband, Milton Fuldheim, died in 1952; within a few years she had remarried a Cleveland businessman, William Ulmer. He in turn died in 1969. In the 1970s she lived with her daughter, Dorothy Louise, whose husband had committed suicide upon returning from World War II, and whose only child, Halla, was permanently disabled with cerebral palsy. Still, this red-haired daughter had fought against tragedy, earned a Ph.D., and got a job teaching literature at Case Western Reserve University. For two years, they shared a newspaper column. Then, in 1980, Dorothy Louise died. Dorothy's world was "blighted." She could never, she wrote, be whole again.

Dorothy Fuldheim's accomplishments were tremendous by any measure. She was the first—and for many years, the only—woman in TV news. She interviewed luminaries as diverse as Einstein, Helen Keller, and Muhammad Ali, and every U.S. president since FDR. She continued to travel abroad to gain important perspectives, from interviewing an IRA hunger striker in Northern Ireland to attending Anwar Sadat's funeral in Cairo, all the while interpreting these complex events for Cleveland viewers. She also took on local issues: traffic, potholes, the court's lack of handicap facilities. In one editorial she spoke of the need for a city ombudsman, presumably because she herself was the one to whom everyone turned with complaints. Glaring at the camera, sometimes shaking her finger, she taught viewers to expect the best from their institutions—and from themselves. Her first sympathies were with the underdog, but she rarely exhibited partisan sympathies and wasn't afraid to describe Jimmy Carter as the dullest man she'd ever interviewed.

On July 26, 1984, at age ninety-one, Dorothy interviewed President Carter's successor, Ronald Reagan, joking with him about trimming fat in the government. Moments after ending the interview, she felt sick and was rushed to the hospital. She had suffered a stroke and underwent emergency surgery. Dorothy spent twelve days in a coma, then miraculously recovered consciousness. When her health permitted, she was moved from the hospital to a nursing home, where she eventually protested her confinement. Her loyal fans protested as well, even picketing the nursing home where she stayed; meanwhile, the *Cleveland Press* ran stories about the loss of freedom incurred by nursing-home residents. Alas, her health did not improve, and she remained in the facility until her death in 1989 at the age of ninety-six. She was memorialized in Cleveland with numerous tributes, both from her own and rival news outlets. Anyone who ever saw her broadcasts remembers Dorothy well.

# BIBLIOGRAPHY

HARRIET BEECHER STOWE

Hedrick, Joan D. *Harriet Beecher Stowe: A Life.* New York: Oxford University Press, 1993.

Stowe, Charles Edward. *Harriet Beecher Stowe: The Story of Her Life.* Boston: Houghton Mifflin Co., 1911.

Stowe, Harriet Beecher. *Uncle Tom's Cabin: Or, Life among the Lowly.* 1952. New York: Modern Library, 2001.

————. *A Key to Uncle Tom's Cabin.* New York: Beaufort Books, 1969.

White, Barbara Ann. *The Beecher Sisters.* New Haven: Yale University Press, 2003.

Wilson, Forrest. *Crusader in Crinoline: the Life of Harriet Beecher Stowe.* Philadelphia: J.B. Lippincott, 1941.

ELIZA JANE TRIMBLE THOMPSON

Bangs, Nathan. *A History of the Methodist Episcopal Church.* 1841. Christian Catholics Ethereal Library at Calvin College. Online: www.ccel.org/b/ bangs/history_mec/

"Crusades" *Woman's Christian Temperance Union.* Online: www.wctu.org/ crusades.html

Smith, S. Winifred. "Allen Trimble." Ohio Historical Society. Online: www. ohiohistory.org/onlinedoc/ohgovernment/governors/trimble.html

Stewart, Eliza Daniel. *Memories of the Crusade, a Thrilling Account of the Great Uprising of the Women of Ohio in 1873, Against the Liquor Crime.* Columbus: Wm. G. Hubbard & Co., 1889.

Thompson, Eliza Jane Trimble. Scrapbook, 1875–1903. Ohio Historical Society Archives.

Thompson, Eliza Jane Trimble et al. Hillsboro Crusade Sketches and Family Records. Ohio Historical Society Archives.

Bibliography

Trimble, John Allen. Family Papers, 1787–1908. Ohio Historical Society Archives.

Tyler, Helen E. *Where Prayer and Purpose Meet: the WCTU Story, 1874–1949.* Evanston, Ill.: The Signal Press, 1949.

Whitaker, Francis Myron. *A History of the Ohio Woman's Christian Temperance Union, 1874–1920.* Dissertation. Ohio State University, 1971.

MARY ANN BALL BICKERDYKE

Baker, Nina Brown. *Cyclone in Calico.* Boston: Little, Brown and Company, 1952.

Chase, Julia A. *Mary A. Bickerdyke, "Mother."* Lawrence, Kans.: Journal Publishing House, 1896.

Erlandson, E. V., "The Story of Mother Bickerdyke," *American Journal of Nursing.* 20:8 (1920).

Livermore, Mary Ashton Rice. *My Story of the War: A Woman's Narrative of Four Years Personal Experience As Nurse in the Union Army and in Relief Work at Home,* (1887) Rpt. Cambridge, Mass.: Da Capo Press, 1995.

VICTORIA C. WOODHULL

Brough, James. *The Vixens: A Biography of Victoria and Tennessee Claflin.* New York: Simon and Schuster, 1980.

Gabriel, Mary. *Notorious Victoria.* Chapel Hill, N.C.: Algonquin Books, 1998.

Goldsmith, Barbara. *Other Powers: The Age of Suffrage, Spiritualism, and the Scandalous Victoria Woodhull.* New York: A. A. Knopf, 1998.

Johnston, Johanna. *Mrs. Satan: The Incredible Saga of Victoria C. Woodhull.* New York: Putnam, 1967.

Sachs, Emanie Nahm. *"The Terrible Siren": Victoria Woodhull.* New York: Harper, 1928.

HALLIE QUINN BROWN

Brown, Hallie Quinn. Papers. Hallie Q. Brown Memorial Library Archives, Central State University.

Bibliography

————. *Homespun Heroines and other Women of Distinction.* 1926. Digital Schomburg African American Women Writers of the Nineteenth Century, New York Public Library. Online: digilib.nypl.org/dynaweb/digs/wwm97253/

Fisher, Vivian Njeri. "Brown, Hallie Quinn." In Darlene Clark Hine, ed. *Black Women in America: A Historical Encyclopedia.* Brooklyn: Carlson Publishing, 1993.

Majors, Monroe A. *Noted Negro Women: Their Triumphs and Activities.* 1893. Freeport, N.Y.: Books for Libraries Press, 1971.

Wesley, Charles H. and Thelma D. Perry. "Hallie Quinn Brown: A Beacon Light." In Daniel, Sadie Iola. *Women Builders.* 2nd edition. Washington, D. C.: Associated Publishers, 1970.

ANNIE OAKLEY

Havighurst, Walter. *Annie Oakley and the Wild West.* New York: Macmillan, 1954.

Kasper, Shirl. *Annie Oakley.* Norman: University of Oklahoma Press, 1992.

Riley, Glenda. *The Life and Legacy of Annie Oakley.* Norman: University of Oklahoma Press, 1994.

Sayers, Isabelle S. *Annie Oakley and Buffalo Bill's Wild West.* New York: Dover Publications, 1981.

HELEN HERRON TAFT

Cordery, Stacy A. "Helen Herron Taft," in *American First Ladies: Their Lives and Their Legacy,* Lewis L. Gould, ed. 2nd ed. New York: Routledge, 2001.

Greenberg, Judith E. *Helen Herron Taft, 1861–1943.* New York: Children's Press, 2000.

Ostromecki, Walter, Jr. "Helen Herron Taft: Influence and Automobiles." *Manuscripts.* 47.3. 1995.

Pringle, Henry F. *The Life and Times of William Howard Taft.* 2 vols. New York: Farrar & Rinehart, 1939.

Roosevelt, Eleanor. "Cherry Blossom Time in Washington." *Reader's Digest.* 32:108 (April 1938) 57–58.

Bibliography

Ross, Ishbel. *An American Family: The Tafts—1678 to 1964.* Cleveland: World Publishing Company, 1964.

Taft, Helen H. *Recollections of Full Years.* New York: Dodd, Mead, 1914.

JANE EDNA HUNTER

Boynton, Virginia R. "Jane Edna Hunter and Black Institution Building in Ohio." *Builders of Ohio.* Warren Van Tine and Michael Pierce, eds. Columbus: Ohio State University Press, 2003.

Daniel, Sadie Iola. *Women Builders.* 2nd ed. Washington, D.C.: Associated Publishers, 1970.

Davis, Russell H. *Black Americans in Cleveland: From George Peake to Carl B. Stokes, 1796–1969.* Washington, D.C.: Associated Publishers, 1972.

Hunter, Jane Edna. *A Nickel and a Prayer.* Cleveland: Elli Kani Publishing Company, 1940.

Jones, Adrienne Lash. *Jane Edna Hunter: A Case Study for Black Leadership, 1910–1950.* Brooklyn, N.Y.: Carlson Publishing Co., 1990.

Phillips, Kimberly L. *Alabama North: African-American Migrants, Community, and Working-Class Activism in Cleveland, 1915–45.* Urbana: University of Illinois Press, 1999.

FLORENCE ELLINWOOD ALLEN

Allen, Florence Ellinwood. *To Do Justly.* Cleveland: Press of Western Reserve University, 1965.

———. *This Constitution of Ours.* New York: G. P. Putnam Sons, 1940.

Russ, John A. "Florence Ellinwood Allen." *Women's Legal History Biography Project.* Online: www.stanford.edu/group/WLHP/papers/flo.html

Tuve, Jeannette E. *First Lady of the Law: Florence Ellinwood Allen.* Lanham, Md.: University Press of America, 1984.

ELLA P. STEWART

Bowers, Ann. "Ella Phillips Stewart." Unpublished. Ella P. Stewart Collection, Center for Archival Collections, Bowling Green State University.

Bibliography

Ella P. Stewart Collection (MS 203). Center for Archival Collections. Bowling Green State University.

Ella P. Stewart Papers. The Ward M. Canaday Center for Special Collections. The University of Toledo.

Rothman, Seymour. "The 'First' Lady." *The Toledo Blade Sunday Magazine.* February 21, 1965.

Smith, Jill Gates. "Ella P. Stewart, PLG." *Women and Health.* 10:4 (Winter, 1986), 3–7.

LOIS LENSKI

Adams, Charles M., ed. *Lois Lenski: An Appreciation.* Greensboro, N.C.: Friends of the Library, Woman's College of the University of North Carolina, 1963.

Day, Pam, Nancy Duran, and Denise Anton Wright. "Books Written and Illustrated by Lois Lenski." Milner Library Special Collections Web site: www.mlb.ilstu.edu/ressubj/speccol/lenski/bib.html.

Lenski, Lois. *Adventure in Understanding: Talks to Parents, Teachers, and Librarians, 1944–1966.* Tallahassee: The Friends of the Florida State University Library, 1968.

———. *Indian Captive: The Story of Mary Jemison.* 1941. New York: HarperCollins, 1994.

———. *Journey Into Childhood: The Autobiography of Lois Lenski.* Philadelphia: J.B. Lippincott Company, 1972.

———. *Prairie School.* Philadelphia: J.B. Lippincott Company, 1951.

———. *Strawberry Girl.* 1945. New York: HarperTrophy, 1995

Schwartz, Vanette. "Biographical Sketch of Lois Lenski." Milner Library Special Collections Web site: www.mlb.ilstu.edu/ressubj/speccol/lenski/History.html

Lovelace, Maud Hart. "Lois Lenski." *Horn Book Magazine.* 22 (1946): 276–82.

DOROTHY FULDHEIM

"Broadcast legend, irrepressible force." *Akron Beacon Journal.* Nov. 4, 1989.

Bibliography

Fuldheim, Dorothy. *A Thousand Friends.* Garden City, N. Y.: Doubleday, 1974.

———. *I Laughed, I Cried, I Loved: A News Analyst's Love Affair with the World.* Cleveland: The World Publishing Company, 1966.

———. Papers, 1968–1990. Kent State University library.

Gray, Nancy. "Before Barbara Walters, There Was Dorothy Fuldheim: Interview." *Ms.* 5 (December 1976), 40.

Mote, Patricia. *Dorothy Fuldheim: The First First Lady of Television News.* Berea, Ohio: Quixote Press, 1997.

Reisman, Judith Ann. *A Rhetorical Analysis of Dorothy Fuldheim's Television Commentaries.* Dissertation. Case Western Reserve University, 1980.

ℐNDEX

Index

Index

Index

Index

About the Author

Greta Anderson grew up in Bexley, Ohio, and attended the Columbus School for Girls. She received a "bicoastal" education in California (B.A.) and New Jersey (M.A., Ph.D), but was glad to return to the Midwest. She now makes her home in Iowa City, Iowa, working as a freelance editor and writer and teaching writing at Kirkwood Community College. She devotes the remainder of her time to political organizing, community literacy programs, her garden, and her dog, Teddy.